YOUR BODY
How It Works

Cells, Tissues, and Skin

YOUR BODY How It Works

Cells, Tissues, and Skin

Douglas Light

Introduction by
Denton A. Cooley, M.D.
President and Surgeon-in-Chief
of the Texas Heart Institute
Clinical Professor of Surgery at the
University of Texas Medical School, Houston, Texas

CHELSEA HOUSE
P U B L I S H E R S
A Haights Cross Communications Company

Philadelphia

CHELSEA HOUSE PUBLISHERS

VP, NEW PRODUCT DEVELOPMENT Sally Cheney
DIRECTOR OF PRODUCTION Kim Shinners
CREATIVE MANAGER Takeshi Takahashi
MANUFACTURING MANAGER Diann Grasse

Staff for CELLS, TISSUES, AND SKIN

EDITOR Beth Reger
PRODUCTION ASSISTANT Megan Emery
PHOTO EDITOR Sarah Bloom
SERIES & COVER DESIGNER Terry Mallon
LAYOUT 21st Century Publishing and Communications, Inc.

A Haights Cross Communications Company

www.chelseahouse.com

First Printing

1 3 5 7 9 8 6 4 2

Library of Congress Cataloging-in-Publication Data applied for.

ISBN 0-7910-7708-X

Table of Contents

Introduction

The human body is an incredibly complex and amazing structure. At best, it is a source of strength, beauty, and wonder. We can compare the healthy body to a well-designed machine whose parts work smoothly together. We can also compare it to a symphony orchestra in which each instrument has a different part to play. When all of the musicians play together, they produce beautiful music.

From a purely physical standpoint, our bodies are made mainly of water. We are also made of many minerals, including calcium, phosphorous, potassium, sulfur, sodium, chlorine, magnesium, and iron. In order of size, the elements of the body are organized into cells, tissues, and organs. Related organs are combined into systems, including the musculoskeletal, cardio-vascular, nervous, respiratory, gastrointestinal, endocrine, and reproductive systems.

Our cells and tissues are constantly wearing out and being replaced without our even knowing it. In fact, much of the time, we take the body for granted. When it is working properly, we tend to ignore it. Although the heart beats about 100,000 times per day and we breathe more than 10 million times per year, we do not normally think about these things. When something goes wrong, however ,our bodies tell us through pain and other symptoms. In fact, pain is a very effective alarm system that lets us know the body needs attention. If the pain does not go away, we may need to see a doctor. Even without medical help, the body has an amazing ability to heal itself. If we cut ourselves, the blood clotting system works to seal the cut right away, and the immune defense system sends out special blood cells that are programmed to heal the area.

During the past 50 years, doctors have gained the ability to repair or replace almost every part of the body. In my own field of cardiovascular surgery, we are able to open the heart and repair its valves, arteries, chambers, and connections. In many cases, these repairs can be done through a tiny "keyhole" incision that speeds up patient recovery and leaves hardly any scar. If the entire heart is diseased, we can replace it altogether, either with a donor heart or with a mechanical device. In the future, the use of mechanical hearts will probably be common in patients who would otherwise die of heart disease.

Until the mid-twentieth century, infections and contagious diseases related to viruses and bacteria were the most common causes of death. Even a simple scratch could become infected and lead to death from "blood poisoning." After penicillin and other antibiotics became available in the 1930s and 40s, doctors were able to treat blood poisoning, tuberculosis, pneumonia, and many other bacterial diseases. Also, the introduction of modern vaccines allowed us to prevent childhood illnesses, smallpox, polio, flu, and other contagions that used to kill or cripple thousands.

Today, plagues such as the "Spanish flu" epidemic of 1918–19 , which killed 20 to 40 million people worldwide, are unknown except in history books. Now that these diseases can be avoided, people are living long enough to have long-term (chronic) conditions such as cancer, heart failure, diabetes, and arthritis. Because chronic diseases tend to involve many organ systems or even the whole body, they cannot always be cured with surgery. These days, researchers are doing a lot of work at the cellular level, trying to find the underlying causes of chronic illnesses. Scientists recently finished mapping the human genome, which is a set of coded "instructions" programmed into our cells. Each cell contains 3 billion "letters" of this code. By showing how the body is made, the human genome will help researchers prevent and treat disease at its source, within the cells themselves.

The body's long-term health depends on many factors, called risk factors. Some risk factors, including our age, sex, and family history of certain diseases, are beyond our control. Other important risk factors include our lifestyle, behavior, and environment. Our modern lifestyle offers many advantages but is not always good for our bodies. In western Europe and the United States, we tend to be stressed, overweight, and out of shape. Many of us have unhealthy habits such as smoking cigarettes, abusing alcohol, or using drugs. Our air, water, and food often contain hazardous chemicals and industrial waste products. Fortunately, we can do something about most of these risk factors. At any age, the most important things we can do for our bodies are to eat right, exercise regularly, get enough sleep, and refuse to smoke, overuse alcohol, or use addictive drugs. We can also help clean up our environment. These simple steps will lower our chances of getting cancer, heart disease, or other serious disorders.

These days, thanks to the Internet and other forms of media coverage, people are more aware of health-related matters. The average person knows more about the human body than ever before. Patients want to understand their medical conditions and treatment options. They want to play a more active role, along with their doctors, in making medical decisions and in taking care of their own health.

I encourage you to learn as much as you can about your body and to treat your body well. These things may not seem too important to you now, while you are young, but the habits and behaviors that you practice today will affect your physical well-being for the rest of your life. The present book series, YOUR BODY: HOW IT WORKS, is an excellent introduction to human biology and anatomy. I hope that it will awaken within you a lifelong interest in these subjects.

Denton A. Cooley, M.D.
President and Surgeon-in-Chief
of the Texas Heart Institute
Clinical Professor of Surgery at the
University of Texas Medical School, Houston, Texas

1

Cells:
The Basis of Life

Cells are the basic units of all living organisms. Some living creatures, such as bacteria and protozoans, consist of only a single cell. In contrast, complex organisms like human beings may be composed of over 75 trillion cells! Just one drop of human blood contains about 5 million red blood cells.

CELLS VARY WIDELY IN SIZE AND SHAPE

Although most cells are microscopic, they vary widely in size. For instance, sperm cells are only about 2 **micrometers** (1/12,000th of an inch) big, whereas some nerve cells are over a meter (3 feet) in length (for example, a single nerve cell connects the spinal cord in your lower back to the little toe).

Cells also vary in shape, which reflects their particular function. *Nerve* cells, for example, have long threadlike extensions that are used to transmit impulses form one part of the body to another. *Epithelial* cells that compose the outer layers of the skin can be flattened and tightly packed like floor tiles, enabling them to protect underlying cells. *Muscle* cells, designed to generate force by contracting, can be slender, rod-shaped structures. Red blood cells, which carry oxygen from the lungs to virtually every cell in the body, are **biconcave** and disk-shaped (Figure 1.1). whereas some kidney cells resemble a cube. All in all, the human body has over 200 different types of cells.

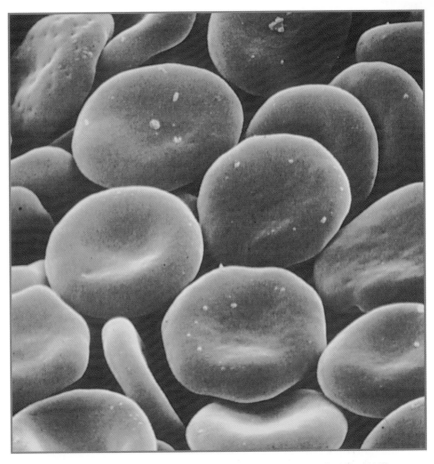

Figure 1.1 There are over 200 different types of cells in the body, and they come in all shapes and sizes. Red blood cells, for example, as pictured here, are biconcave disks. This unique shape allows them to efficiently carry oxygen for distribution throughout the body.

THE DISCOVERY OF CELLS

Because of their small size, the discovery of cells and their structure had to wait for the invention of the microscope. During the mid-seventeenth century, the English scientist Robert Hooke looked at thinly sliced cork with a simple microscope. He observed tiny compartments, which he termed "*cellulae*," the Latin word for small rooms; hence the origin of the biological term *cell* (technically speaking, he actually observed the walls of dead plant cells, but no one at that time thought of cells as being dead or alive). In the late seventeenth century, the Dutch shopkeeper Anton van Leeuwenhoek constructed lenses that provided clarity and magnification not previously possible. With these new lenses, he observed very small "*animalcules*" from scrapings of tartar from his own teeth, as well as **protozoans** from a variety of water samples.

In the early nineteenth century, the German botanist

WHY ARE CELLS SMALL?

Why are most cells microscopic in size? It turns out that there are physical constraints placed on cells, which are determined by their *surface area-to-volume ratio*. This is because an object's volume increases with the cube of its diameter. However, the surface area only increases with the square of the diameter. In other words, as a cell grows in size, the volume increases faster than the surface area. For example, if a cell grows four times in diameter, then its volume would increase by 64 times (4^3), whereas its surface area only by 16 times (4^2). In this example, the plasma membrane would therefore have to serve four times as much cytoplasm as it did previously. Thus, if a cell were to grow unchecked, it would soon reach a point where the inward flow of nutrients and outward flow of waste products across the plasma membrane would not occur at a rate sufficient to keep the cell alive.

The importance of a large surface area for cells also is seen by the numerous in-foldings and out-foldings in the plasma membrane of many cell types. These folds dramatically increase the surface area relative to cell volume. This is especially important for cells that absorb large quantities of substances, such as those lining the small intestine and many cells in the kidneys.

Matthias Schleiden, who also studied cells with a microscope, proposed that the nucleus might have something to do with cell development. During the same time period, the German zoologist Theodor Schwann theorized that animals and plants consist of cells, and that cells have an individual life of their own. Rudolf Virchow, a German physiologist who studied cell growth and reproduction, suggested all cells come from pre-existing cells. His proposal was actually revolutionary for the time because it challenged the widely accepted theory of **spontaneous generation**, which held that living organisms arise spontaneously from nonliving material, such as garbage.

By the middle of the nineteenth century, the scientific community developed several generalizations, which today we term the **cell theory**. The cell theory includes three important principles. First, every living organism is composed of one or more cells. Second, cells are the smallest units that have the properties of life. Third, the continuity of life has a cellular basis.

Microscopes

Modern microscopes have dramatically increased our ability to observe cell structure. Light microscopes use two or more sets of highly polished glass lenses to bend light rays to illuminate

CELL THEORY

The cell theory, developed in the mid-nineteenth century, provided scientists with a clearer insight of the study of life. The cell theory involves the following three aspects:

1. Every living organism is composed of one or more cells.

2. Cells are the smallest units that have the properties of life.

3. The continuity of life has a cellular basis.

a specimen, thereby enlarging its image. Consequently, in order to be seen, a specimen must be thin enough for light to pass through it. Also, cells are 60-80% water, which is colorless and clear. This, in turn, makes it difficult to observe the various unpigmented structures of cells. This problem is overcome by exposing cells to a **stain** (dye), which colors some cell parts, but not others.

Unfortunately, staining usually kills cells. However, there are several types of microscopes designed to use *phase-contrast* or *Nomarksi optics*, which use light refraction to create contrast without staining. For instance, with Nomarski optics, a prism is used to split a beam of polarized light in two and project both beams through a specimen at slightly different angles. When the beams are later combined, they exhibit bright and dark interference patterns that highlight areas in cells that have differing thicknesses. These specialized optics obviously enhance the usefulness of light microscopes.

Two factors need to be considered when discussing microscopy: a microscope's ability to *magnify* images and its ability to *resolve* them. **Magnification** simply means making an image appear larger in size. **Resolution** refers to the ability to make separate parts look clear and distinguishable from one another, which becomes increasingly more difficult as magnification increases. Consequently, if a microscope magnified an image without providing sufficient resolution, the image would appear large but unclear.

Light microscopes have an inherent limitation regarding resolution because of the physical nature of light. Light, a form of **electromagnetic radiation**, has wave-like properties, where the wavelength refers to the distance between two wave crests (red light, for example, has a longer wavelength than violet light; 750 **nanometers** versus 400 nanometers, respectively). Therefore, if a cell structure is less than one-half the wavelength of illuminating light, it will not be able to disturb the light rays streaming past it. In other words, it will be invisible. As a result, light microscopes are not useful for observing objects smaller than several hundred nanometers.

Electron microscopes have a much greater resolving power because they use a beam of electrons to "illuminate" a specimen instead of light. Although electrons are particles, they also have wave-like properties, and a stream of electrons has a wavelength about 100,000 times shorter than that of visible light. This allows an electron microscope to resolve images down to about 0.5 nanometers in size. Because a beam of electrons cannot pass through glass, its path is focused by a magnetic field. In addition, specimens must be placed in a vacuum, otherwise molecules of air would deflect the electron beam.

There are two main kinds of electron microscopes. A **transmission electron microscope** (Figure 1.2) accelerates a beam of electrons through a specimen, which allows internal structures within a cell to be imaged. In contrast, a **scanning electron microscope** moves a narrow beam of electrons across a specimen that has been coated with a thin layer of metal. This method is ideally suited for imaging the surface of a specimen (Figure 1.3).

CHEMICAL CONSTITUENTS OF CELLS

Chemically, cells are mainly composed of four **elements**: carbon, hydrogen, oxygen, and nitrogen. Although these four **major elements** make up over 95% of a cell's structure, the lesser abundant **trace elements** also are important for certain cell functions (Figure 1.4). Iron, for instance, is needed to make *hemoglobin*, which carries oxygen in the blood. Blood clotting, and the proper formation of bones and teeth all require calcium. Iodine is necessary to make thyroid hormone, which controls the body's metabolic rate. A lack of iodine in the diet can lead to the formation of a

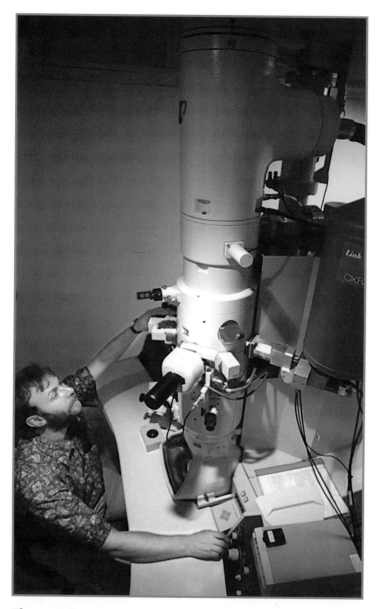

Figure 1.2 A transmission electron microscope (TEM) utilizes a beam of electrons to allow scientists to visualize the internal components of a cell. In addition, TEMs provide much greater resolution (clarity) and magnification than traditional light microscopes. The TEM pictured here is located at the University of New Mexico.

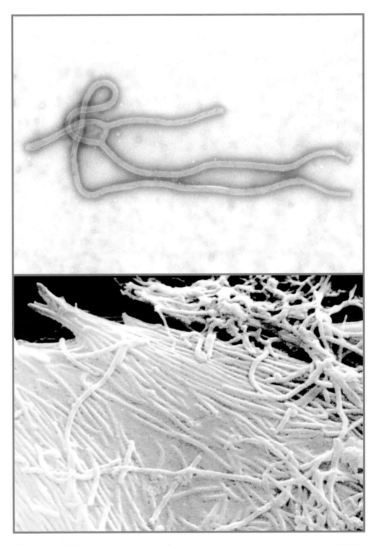

Figure 1.3 Like TEMs, scanning electron microscopes, or SEMs, utilize a beam of electrons to visualize specimens. However, SEMs provide a picture of the outside structure of a specimen, rather than its internal components. Pictured here are specimens of the Ebola virus. The picture on the top was taken with a transmission electron microscope. Note that the cell appears translucent and the inner components are visible. The picture on the bottom was taken with a scanning electron microscope, and only the surface of the specimen is visible.

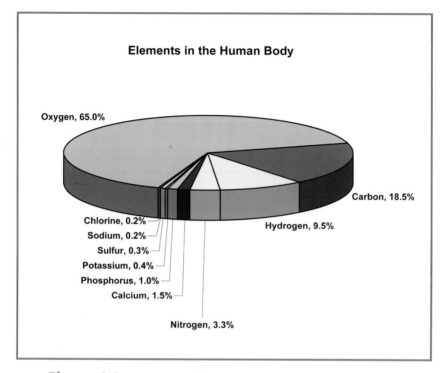

Figure 1.4 Oxygen, carbon, hydrogen, and nitrogen are all important components of cells and make up over 90% of a cell's structure. Calcium, phosphorus, and potassium are also found in cells, but in much smaller amounts and are known as trace elements. Figure 1.4 shows some of the more common elements found in cells and their approximate amounts.

goiter (an enlarged thyroid gland). Although goiters were relatively common in the past, they are less common today because dietary iodine can be obtained through the consumption of iodized salt. Sodium and potassium are also necessary elements, especially for the transmission of nerve impulses and for muscle contraction.

It is convenient to divide the chemicals that enter cells or are produced by them into two main groups: **organic** substances (those that contain carbon and hydrogen atoms), and **inorganic** substances (all the rest). The most abundant inorganic molecule in cells (and the entire body) is water. In fact, it accounts for about two-thirds of an adult human's weight. This helps explain why water is essential for life. Water is important as a **solvent** because many substances (**solutes**) dissolve in it. Also, water helps stabilize body temperature because, compared to most fluids, it can absorb a lot of heat before its temperature rises, and cells release a great amount of heat during normal **metabolism** (the sum total of all the chemical reactions taking place in the body). In addition to water, other inorganic substances found in cells include oxygen, carbon dioxide, and numerous inorganic salts, such as sodium chloride (ordinary table salt).

Organic substances in cells include **carbohydrates**, **lipids**, **proteins**, and nucleic acids. Carbohydrates, such as sugars and glycogen, provide much of the energy that cells require. Carbohydrates also provide materials to build certain cell structures. Lipids include compounds such as fats (primarily used to store energy), phospholipids (an important constituent of cell membranes), and cholesterol (used to synthesize steroid hormones, such as testosterone and estrogen). Proteins serve as structural materials and an energy source. In addition, most enzymes and many hormones are composed of protein. **Nucleic acids** form the genes found in DNA and also take part in protein synthesis.

STRUCTURE OF A GENERALIZED CELL

Although cells differ in many respects, they all have certain characteristics and structures in common. Consequently, it is possible to construct a generalized or *composite* cell (Figure 1.5). For human beings, our cells typically start out with three structures in common. They all have a **plasma membrane,** the thin outer boundary that separates the intracellular environment from the extracellular one. The plasma membrane therefore maintains cells as distinct entities. In doing so, plasma membranes also allow specific chemical reactions to occur inside the cell separate from random events in the environment.

Human cells also typically have a **nucleus.** There is one notable exception, however. Mature red blood cells do not possess a nucleus. The nucleus contains heritable genetic material called **deoxyribonucleic acid** (**DNA**) and molecules of **ribonucleic acid** (**RNA**) that are able to copy instructions from DNA.

In addition, cells contain a semi-fluid **cytoplasm.** It surrounds the nucleus and is encircled by the plasma membrane. Cytoplasm contains specialized structures suspended in a liquid **cytosol** called **organelles,** which perform specific cell functions. Whereas organelles divide the labor of a cell, the nucleus directs overall cell activities.

Levels of Structural Organization

Single-celled organisms (*protozoans*) have the ability to carry out all necessary life functions as individual cells. For example, they can obtain and digest food, eliminate waste products, and respond to a number of different stimuli. However, in multicellular organisms, such as human beings, cells do not generally operate independently. Instead, they display highly specialized functions, and only by living and communicating with other cells, do they allow the entire organisms to survive.

Groups of cells that are similar in structure and perform a common or related function are called **tissues.** There are four main tissue types in the human body (*epithelial, connective, muscle,* and *nervous*), and each performs a different role (a further discussion of tissues is presented in Chapter 6). The study of tissues is called **histology,** and physicians who specialize in this field are called pathologists (histologists). These doctors often remove tissues from a patient during an operation or from a person during a post-mortem examination,

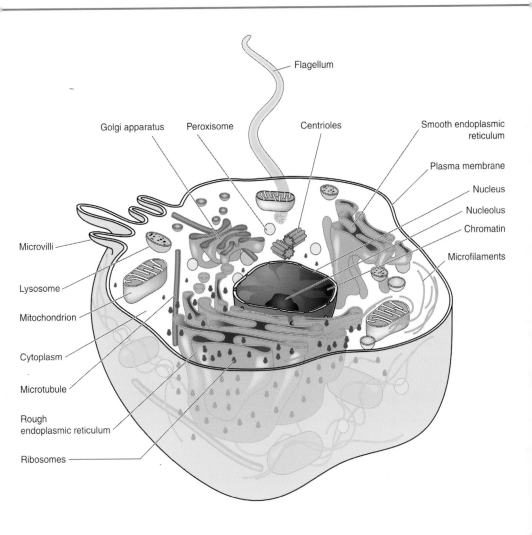

Figure 1.5 Cells are the smallest units of life, and all living organisms are composed of one or more cells. This figure of a composite cell illustrates some of the common features and organization of many cell types. However, it does not do justice to the tremendous diversity in size, shape, and structure of cells, which reflect their different functions. Note the various components within a cell, which perform specific functions, thereby allowing the cell to survive and perform particular tasks.

and look at the cells with a microscope to help diagnose the presence of specific diseases. Cancer, for instance, is detected in this manner.

Tissues can be organized into more complex structures called **organs,** which perform specific functions for the body. Some examples of organs include the kidneys, lungs, stomach, liver, and skin (the skin will be discussed in later chapters). Many organs, such as the small intestine and skin, are composed of all four tissue types. The small intestine, for instance, is capable of digesting and absorbing food, which requires the cooperation of a number of different kinds of cells and tissue types.

A **system** is considered a group of organs that cooperate to accomplish a common purpose. An example is the digestive system, which contains a number of organs, including the esophagus, stomach, and small intestine. The **integumentary system** (skin and its accessory structures) is discussed in Chapter 7. All the organ systems of the body make up the complete organism.

CONNECTIONS

Cells are the basic units of all living organisms. Although most cells are microscopic, they vary widely in size. Cells also vary in shape, which reflects their particular function. Through investigation of cells, scientists have developed the cell theory, which proposes that all living organisms are composed of one or more cells, cells are the smallest units that have the properties of life, and the continuity of life has a cellular basis.

Chemically, cells are mainly composed of four elements (carbon, hydrogen, oxygen, and nitrogen) and some trace elements (sodium, potassium, calcium, and iron). The most abundant inorganic molecule in cells is water. Organic substances in cells include carbohydrates, lipids, proteins, and nucleic acids. In addition, all human cells start out with three structures in common: a plasma membrane, a nucleus, and cytoplasmic organelles.

Groups of cells that are similar in structure and perform a common or related function are called tissues. Tissues can be organized into more complex structures called organs, which perform specific functions for the body. A system is considered a group of organs that cooperate to accomplish a common purpose, and all the organ systems of the body make up the complete organism.

2

Cell Membranes:
Ubiquitous Biological Barriers

A cell membrane called the **plasma membrane** surrounds every single cell—there are no exceptions. It encircles a cell, thereby forming a barrier containing the cytoplasm within, and separating cellular contents from the surrounding environment. In addition, nearly all types of organelles are enclosed by a similar cell membrane. Regardless of location, cell membranes are much more than simple boundaries. In fact, they are an actively functioning part of living cells, and many important chemical reactions take place on their inner and outer surfaces (Figure 2.1).

GENERALIZED CHARACTERISTICS OF CELL MEMBRANES
In spite of their extreme importance, cell membranes are actually quite fragile and thin. They are typically 7–8 nanometers thick (about 10,000 times thinner than a strand of hair), and thus are only visible with the aid of an electron microscope. In addition to maintaining cell integrity, the plasma membrane also controls the movement of most substances that enter and exit a cell. Because cell membranes have the ability to let some items through but not others, they are referred to as **selectively permeable** (also known as **semipermeable**). The permeability properties of the plasma membrane depend on a healthy, intact cell. When cells are damaged, their membranes may become leaky to virtually everything, allowing substances to freely flow across them. For instance, when a person has been severely burned, there can be significant

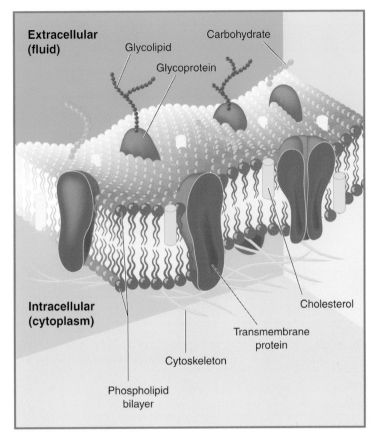

Figure 2.1 The plasma membrane of a cell protects the cell and also serves as a "doorway" to allow certain components into and out of the cell. It is composed of a phospholipid bilayer containing cholesterol, glycolipids, carbohydrates, and protein molecules.

loss of fluids, proteins, and ions from dead and damaged cells in the burned areas.

Membrane Structure

Cell membranes have a tall order to fill. Not only must they provide a structurally stable boundary, they also need to be flexible and semipermeable. For these reasons, the basic structural framework of all cell membranes is a double layer (called a **bilayer**) of **phospholipid** molecules (Figure 2.2), with protein and **cholesterol** molecules dispersed within the layers.

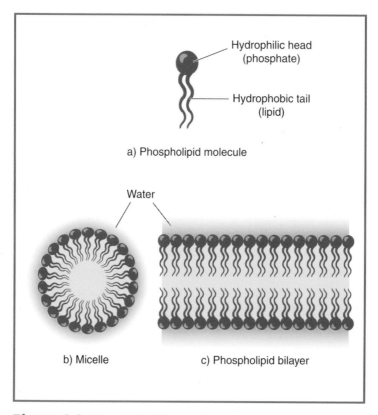

Figure 2.2 Phospholipids are the main components of a cell membrane. They allow for both flexibility and support. A phospholipid is composed of a phosphate group, two fatty acid chains, and a glyercol molecule. The polar, hydrophilic heads of the molecule, made up of the phosphate groups, point towards the inner and outer surfaces of the cell while the fatty acid tails are hydrophobic and reside on the inside of the membrane.

A close inspection of the structural properties of phospholipid molecules is key to understanding how a lipid bilayer forms and how it provides a structurally stable boundary. Each phospholipid molecule has a **phosphate** group and two **fatty acids** chains bound to a three-carbon *glycerol* molecule (a 3-carbon sugar alcohol that contains three hydroxyl groups), making the whole thing look like a lollipop with two sticks.

Phosphate groups are **polar** (meaning charged), making the end of the phospholipid molecule **hydrophilic** (water-soluble). In contrast, the fatty acid regions are **nonpolar** (that is, uncharged), rendering the other portion of the phospholipid **hydrophobic** (water insoluble).

Because water is a major component of both cytoplasm and extracellular fluid, the polar phosphate groups orient themselves so that they lie on both the inner and outer surfaces of a bilayer. In contrast, the nonpolar fatty acid "tails" avoid water by lining up in the center of the membrane, sandwiched between the polar "heads." The result is a bilayer composed of two parallel sheets of phospholipid molecules arranged as mirror images. In this way, the two layers lie tail-to-tail, exposing the polar heads to water. This self-orienting property of phospholipids in an aqueous environment allows cell membranes to self-assemble and also to repair themselves quickly.

About 10% of the outer facing layer of the membrane is composed of **glycolipids**, lipids with sugar groups attached to them. In addition, about 20% of the lipid in membranes is cholesterol. This molecule stabilizes the overall structure of a membrane by wedging itself between the phospholipid tails. This also makes membranes less fluid.

A lipid bilayer structure is well suited to provide a structurally stable, flexible barrier that is relatively impermeable to most water-soluble substances. However, cells also must acquire water-soluble nutrients found in the surrounding environment. In addition, cells need to eliminate water-soluble waste products. These problems are overcome by the presence of proteins scattered in the lipid bilayer. In fact, proteins make up about half of membranes by weight, and are responsible for most of their specialized functions. In other words, the lipid portion of most membranes is essentially the same; and it is the presence of specific proteins that gives each membrane its specific properties.

Membrane Proteins

There are two distinct populations of membrane proteins: **integral** and **peripheral**. Integral proteins are inserted into the lipid bilayer; most are *transmembrane*, meaning they span the entire width of the membrane, protruding on both sides. Integral proteins are mainly involved with transport functions (described below). In contrast, peripheral proteins are attached on either the inner or outer surface of the membrane. These proteins often serve as **enzymes** or in mechanical functions, such as changing cell shape during cell division or in muscle contraction. Based on its overall structure, the **fluid mosaic model** is used to describe biological membranes because the lipid portion has fluid-like properties, whereas proteins are dispersed within it forming a mosaic-like pattern.

Many proteins on the extracellular side of membranes have attached sugar residues and are described as **glycoproteins.** The term **glycocalyx** ("cell coat") refers to the fuzzy carbohydrate-rich area on cell surfaces. The glycocalyx is significant because it provides highly specific biological markers, which can be recognized by other cells. For example, white blood cells of our immune system identify "self-cells" of the body from invading bacterial cells by binding to certain membrane glycoproteins. In addition, sperm recognize an ovum by the egg's unique glycocalyx. The glycocalyx on red blood cells is what determines blood type. Unfortunately, continuous changes in the glycocalyx occur when cells become cancerous. This in turn allows cancer cells to evade the immune system and avoid destruction.

Functions of Membrane Proteins

Membrane proteins serve a variety of important functions, giving properties to cell membranes that otherwise would not be possible. Most notably, transmembrane proteins mediate the movement of substances into and out of cells (described in further detail in the next section). Membrane proteins also serve as **enzymes**, molecules that increase the rate of chemical reactions. In addition, membrane proteins exposed to the outside surface of cells may act as **receptors**. A receptor is a molecule with a binding site that fits the specific shape of a particular chemical messenger, such as a hormone. In this way, chemical messages released by one cell type can communicate with another cell type, thereby influencing its activity. In a similar manner, some glycoproteins on the outer cell surface serve as identification tags that are specifically recognized by other cell proteins in a process called **cell-cell recognition**.

In addition, membrane proteins of adjacent cells may be linked together. These **cell adhesion molecules** (CAMs) provide temporary binding sites that guide cell migration, or they may provide more permanent attachments between cells. Unfortunately, CAMs often are not expressed in cancer cells. This explains why cells from a **tumor** may separate and spread to other locations in the body; a process known as **metastasis**. Finally, some membrane proteins provide attachment sites for the **cytoskeleton** (an internal support system, described in Chapter 3) and the **extracellular matrix** (nonliving material secreted by cells, described in Chapter 5). These membrane proteins are important for helping maintain cell shape. They also help anchor and thereby fix the location of certain proteins within the fluid-like membrane.

DIFFUSION

Diffusion is the process by which particles spread spontaneously from regions of higher concentration towards regions where they are of lower concentration. All atoms and molecules contain *kinetic energy* obtained from heat in the environment. Consequently, they are in constant motion. As they move about randomly at high speeds, they collide and ricochet off one another, changing direction with each collision (that is why diffusion is referred to as *random thermal motion* and why diffusion would cease to occur at absolute zero, -273°C).

The overall effect of random thermal motion is that

particles move away from areas of higher concentration, where collisions are more frequent, to areas of lower concentration (Figure 2.3). In this manner, particles are said to diffuse "down" their **concentration gradient**. In a closed system, diffusion will eventually produce a uniform distribution of

WHY WE CANNOT SURVIVE BY DIFFUSION ALONE.

Diffusion causes individual molecules to travel at high velocities. For example, thermal motion of water molecules at body temperature is approximately 2500 km/hr (about 1500 mph). Surprisingly, however, the rate of movement from one location to another by diffusion is actually slow for distances much further than about the size of a cell. This is because individual molecules cannot travel very far before bumping into another. In water, for instance, there is a collision about every about 0.3 nanometers, and the constant bumping of molecules alters their direction of movement with each collision. Therefore, although individual molecules travel at high velocities, the number of collisions they undergo prevents them from traveling very far in a straight line. Consequently, diffusion can distribute molecules rapidly over short distances (within the cytoplasm or between a few layers of cells), but is extremely slow over distances greater than a few centimeters.

As an illustration of the above concept, spray a small amount of perfume in the front of a classroom, and time how long it takes for students in the back of the room to smell it. It will likely be within a few minutes. Was that spread of perfume to the back of the room due to diffusion? Based on what you know about this process, your answer should be no. In fact, depending on the size of the room, it would likely take 15–20 days for molecules of perfume to reach the back by diffusion. Why then can perfume be smelled after only a few minutes? The answer is, perfume molecules are carried by wind currents in a process known as **bulk flow**.

particles, which is called a state of **equilibrium**. Although particles continue to move and collide after equilibrium is achieved, their concentration gradients no longer change because the particles move equally in all directions (i.e., there is no "net" movement).

Another example to illustrate this process involves distribution of oxygen within the body after it has reached the lungs. By diffusion alone, it would take over 200 days for oxygen to travel from your lungs to your brain (keep in mind, brain cells die within 4–6 minutes in the absence of oxygen). In contrast, oxygen diffuses to the center of a single-celled protozoan in about 20 milliseconds. Although the one-celled protozoan can rely on diffusion alone for gas exchange, we cannot because we are physically too large (surface area to volume constraints are described in chapter 1). However, our blood stream solves this problem by moving oxygen (and other substances) around the body much more quickly than diffusion.

Based on what you know about diffusion, what can you predict about the distance between body tissues and near-by capillaries? Hint, if a capillary and a muscle cell were only separated by 10 centimeters (about 4 inches), it would take over 11 years for glucose to diffuse that distance! Obviously, the distance is much less than that, which helps explain why capillaries are so small (so they can be within diffusing distance of virtually every cell in your body).

As a general rule, diffusion is an efficient way to move substances across cell membranes. In fact, diffusion is the mechanism by which oxygen molecules cross lung tissue to enter the blood stream and how oxygen leaves capillaries to enter body tissues. In contrast, bulk flow mechanisms are necessary to carry substances from one part of the body to another. For example, bulk flow is how air is brought into the lungs from the atmosphere when we inhale.

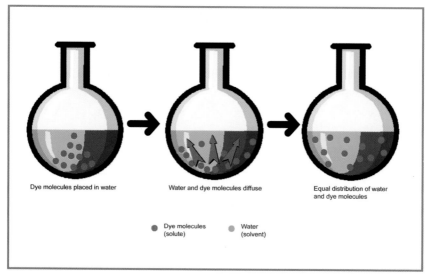

Figure 2.3 **A high concentration of a water-soluble substance will eventually become equally distributed throughout a solution by diffusion. Diffusion is a process whereby random thermal motion distributes particles from regions of higher concentration to those of lower concentration. Although not readily visible, water molecules also undergo random thermal motion. As can be seen in this diagram, dye molecules will randomly distribute throughout the water. Once the dye and water molecules are evenly distributed (equilibrium), diffusion of both molecules continues, but at equal rates in all directions.**

CONNECTIONS

The plasma membrane is an actively functioning part of living cells. In addition to maintaining cell integrity, it also controls movement of substances that enter and exit cells. Most organelles also are surrounded by a membrane. All cell membranes are composed of a phospholipid bilayer, with protein and cholesterol molecules dispersed within the layers. Membrane proteins serve a variety of diverse functions. For instance, they transport substances into and out of cells and also serve as cell-cell recognition sites. In addition, membrane proteins act as enzymes, receptors, and cell adhesion molecules.

Diffusion is the process by which particles spread spontaneously from regions of higher concentration towards regions where they are of lower concentration. In this manner, particles are said to diffuse "down" their concentration gradient. Although individual molecules travel at high velocities, the number of collisions they undergo prevents them from traveling very far in a straight line. Consequently, diffusion can distribute molecules rapidly over short distances (within the cytoplasm or between a few layers of cells), but is extremely slow over distances greater than a few centimeters.

3

Movement Through Cell Membranes:
How to Cross a Barrier

The cell membrane is a selective barrier that controls movement of substances that both enter and leave cells. Many of these movements involve **passive transport** processes (not requiring cellular energy), such as *simple diffusion, facilitated diffusion, osmosis,* and *filtration.* In contrast, **active transport** mechanisms require cellular energy in the form of **ATP**. This includes transport by *solute pumps* and the processes of *endocytosis* and *exocytosis.*

PASSIVE MECHANISMS

The unassisted diffusion of lipid soluble solutes through the plasma membrane is called **simple diffusion**. Such substances include oxygen, carbon dioxide, fat-soluble vitamins, and alcohol. These nonpolar substances are capable of passing through the hydrophobic interior of the plasma membrane. Their direction of net flow will depend on the concentration gradient. For example, the concentration of oxygen molecules is always higher in the blood than in cells, so it continuously enters cells by simple diffusion. The opposite is true for carbon dioxide (Figure 3.1).

Most water-soluble substances, however, are unable to diffuse through the lipid portion of a membrane. In this case, special transmembrane proteins shaped like hollow cylinders, called

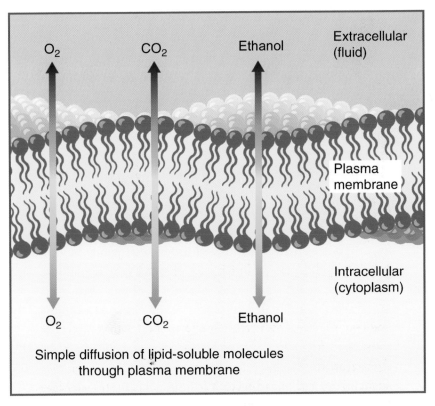

Figure 3.1 The cell membrane is selectively permeable, meaning it only lets specific substances pass. Fat-soluble substances, such as oxygen (O_2), carbon dioxide (CO_2), and alcohol, may pass through a cell membrane unassisted by the process of simple diffusion because they can dissolve in the lipid bilayer.

channels, are utilized. Because these proteins are filled with water, they create an aqueous pore that traverses the entire thickness of a membrane. Like a highway tunnel through a mountain for automobiles, channels provide a pathway for small polar particles to diffuse through the membrane. Movement through channels is passive because it does not require energy from cells and simply depends on the concentration gradient.

Under most circumstances, it would not be useful for a channel to be open all the time. That is why channels are "*gated*," which means they have the ability to open and close in response to appropriate chemical or electrical signals. Although the sizes of channel pores vary, they are typically on the order of nanometers in diameter. Channel pores also tend to be very selective as to what they will allow to pass through. Most channels are primarily permeable to a specific ion, such as to sodium, potassium, calcium, or chloride.

Certain molecules, such as glucose, amino acids, and urea, are too polar to dissolve in the lipid bilayer and they also are too large to pass through channels. However, they do move rapidly through the plasma membrane. This is accomplished by a passive process called **facilitated diffusion**. In this case, the transported substance moves across the membrane by interacting with a protein "**carrier**" molecule. Although movement by facilitated diffusion follows a concentration gradient, the carrier is needed as a transport "vehicle" to allow a substance to cross the lipid bilayer. If you think of an ion channel as a typical door in a classroom, then a carrier protein could be thought of as a revolving door in a department store. In other words, unlike the channel that has a continuous tunnel traversing a membrane, a carrier appears to have a binding site that is moved from one face of the membrane

YOUR HEALTH: Cystic Fibrosis

Mutations that effect channel selectively or their regulation can have serious health consequences. For example, cystic fibrosis, the most common inherited disorder among Caucasians, results from a malfunctioning chloride channel, which causes abnormal secretion in *exocrine* glands. As a result, this disease causes the respiratory tract to fill with abnormally thick mucus, as well as preventing the pancreas from properly producing digestive enzymes. Defective ion channels also are responsible for diseases that lead to improper rhythm of the heart, high blood pressure, low blood sugar from excessive insulin secretion, and several neurological disorders.

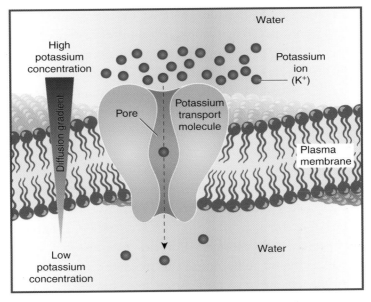

Figure 3.2 Most water-soluble substances are unable to diffuse through a lipid bilayer (as shown here). However, small polar or charged particles (such as water and ions) can cross a cell membrane by diffusing through protein structures called *channels*, which form water-filled pores that traverse the width of a membrane. This figure illustrates potassium ions diffusing through a potassium-permeable channel. Lipid-insoluble substances that are too large to permeate channel proteins (e.g., glucose and amino acids) may cross a cell membrane using protein *carrier* molecules in a process known as facilitated diffusion (see text for a further explanation of this process).

to the other by conformational changes in the protein. In addition, as with channels, carriers tend to be highly selective as to what they will transport (Figure 3.2).

Osmosis is a special case of diffusion. It occurs when water molecules diffuse from a region of higher water concentration to a region of lower concentration across a selectively permeable membrane (Figure 3.3). In solutions, solute takes up space that water molecules would otherwise occupy. Thus, a higher concentration of solute means a lower concentration of water. The extent to which the water concentration is decreased by solute particles depends only on their number and not their size, kind, or charge. For example, if distilled water were on both sides of a selectively permeable membrane, no net osmosis would occur. However, if the solute concentration on two sides of a membrane differed, the water concentration also would differ. Water would then diffuse across the membrane from the region of lower solute concentration towards the region of higher solute concentration.

The flow of water across a membrane by osmosis can change the volume on both sides. Consequently, the movement of water into a closed system, such as a cell, will exert pressure against the plasma membrane, which is referred to as **osmotic pressure**. Osmotic imbalances (differences in the total solute concentration on both sides of a membrane) would therefore cause animal cells to swell or shrink, due to net water gain or loss. In this case, cells will continue to change size until they reach equilibrium; that is, the solute concentration is the same on both sides of the plasma membrane. Alternatively, before equilibrium is reached, a cell could swell until it bursts. The concentration of water and solutes everywhere inside the body must therefore be regulated so it is the same on both sides of cell membranes in order to keep cells from changing their

YOUR HEALTH: Regarding Osmosis

Osmosis is an important consideration when health care providers give intravenous solutions to patients. For example, if a treatment is designed to infuse patients with solutions that have the same solute and water concentration as body cells, then an isotonic solution would need to be used. However, sometimes hypertonic solutions are given to patients who have swollen feet and hands due to fluid retention. Such solutions draw water out of the tissue spaces into the bloodstream so it can be eliminated by the kidneys. In contrast, hypotonic solutions may be infused to rehydrate tissues of extremely dehydrated patients.

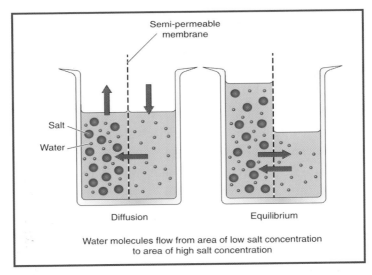

Semi-permeable
membrane

Salt

Water

Diffusion   Equilibrium

Water molecules flow from area of low salt concentration
to area of high salt concentration

Figure 3.3 In this system, the membrane separating these two solutions is permeable to water but not to solute (salt). As a consequence, water will move by osmosis from the compartment containing a lower solute concentration (right side) to the solution with a higher solute concentration (left side) until equilibrium is reached. Note that as a result of water flow across the membrane, the volume of the right compartment decreased.

volume. In fact, a major function of the kidneys is to maintain the volume and composition of the extracellular fluid constant by modifying the volume and composition of urine.

Solutions that have the same osmotic pressure as cells and body fluids are considered **isotonic**, and they do not cause cells to change size. In contrast, a solution with a higher osmotic pressure than body fluids is **hypertonic**. Cells placed in a hypertonic medium will shrink due to the net movement of water out of the cell into the surrounding medium. On the other hand, cells exposed to a **hypotonic** solution, which has a lower osmotic pressure than body fluids, will gain water by osmosis and swell. In fact, under some hypotonic conditions, cells swell to the point of breaking, analogous to a balloon that is over-inflated with air (Figure 3.4).

In some instances, water and solute particles are forced through membranes by **hydrostatic pressure**. This process is called **filtration**. The force for this movement usually comes from blood pressure, which is created largely by the pumping action of the heart. Like diffusion, filtration across a membrane is a passive process. However, in this case the driving force is a pressure gradient that actually pushes solute-containing fluid from the higher-pressure area to a lower-pressure area. An example of this is filtration of blood in the kidneys, which is the first step in urine formation.

ACTIVE MECHANISMS

Sometimes particles move across cell membranes against their concentration gradients: that is from regions of lower concentration to ones of higher concentration. This type of movement is called active transport, and it requires cells to use energy in the form of ATP. Substances moved across a membrane in this manner are usually unable to pass in the necessary direction by any of the passive processes. For example, they may be too large to traverse channels and carriers, they may not dissolve in the lipid bilayer, or they may have to move "uphill" against their concentration gradients. It is estimated that up to 40% of a cell's energy supply is used for active transport of particles through membranes. There are two major mechanisms of transport that require ATP: *solute pumping* and *vesicular transport.*

Solute pumping (also called *active transport*) is similar to facilitated diffusion in that it uses specific carrier molecules in the cell membrane. That is, these protein molecules have binding sites that combine temporarily and specifically with the particles being transported. However, whereas facilitated diffusion is driven by the kinetic energy of the diffusing particles, solute pumps use ATP. Because this type of transport moves substances against their

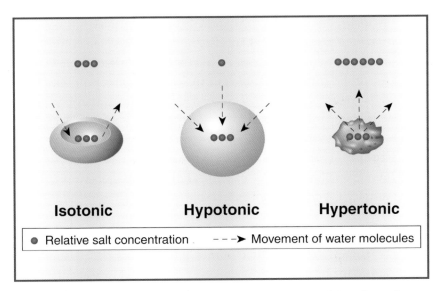

Isotonic   **Hypotonic**   **Hypertonic**

● Relative salt concentration   - - -➤ Movement of water molecules

Figure 3.4 This figure shows a diagrammatic view of the effect of different solutions on living cells. Isotonic solutions have the same concentration of non-penetrating solutes as inside cells. Under these conditions, cells retain their normal size and shape. However, cells gain water and swell when exposed to hypotonic conditions. This results because the concentration of non-penetrating solutes in hypotonic solutions is less than in cells, which generates a driving force for water to flow into cells by osmosis. In contrast, hypertonic solutions contain more non-penetrating solutes than inside cells, which causes cells to shrink due to the loss of water.

concentration gradients, the carrier proteins are referred to as *pumps*.

The most ubiquitous active transport carrier is the *sodium-potassium pump*. This protein transports sodium ions out of the cell, while simultaneously moving potassium ions in the other direction. Consequently, it keeps intracellular sodium levels low, while also keeping intracellular levels of potassium relatively high (about 10-20 times greater than what is found in the extracellular fluid). These artificial concentration gradients maintained by the pump are necessary for nerve and muscles cells to function normally, and also for body cells to maintain their normal fluid volumes. Because there is a continual "leak" of sodium into cells by diffusion, as well as a leak of potassium in the other direction, this pump operates more or less continuously. The pump also can change its rate of transport, depending on the level of sodium and potassium leak (which, for example, temporarily increases during a nerve impulse or muscle contraction when there is a transient increase in membrane leak for sodium and potassium). Another example of active transport includes a potassium-hydrogen pump found in stomach cells, which is used to form hydrochloric acid.

Some substances that cannot move across the plasma membrane by any other means are transported by **vesicular transport. Endocytosis** ("into a cell") describes vesicular transport where particles are brought into a cell by engulfing or enclosing them within small membranous **vesicles**. Once a vesicle is formed, it detaches from the plasma membrane and moves into the cytoplasm, where it often fuses with a cellular organelle that contains digestive enzymes (Figure 3.5). This mechanisms is well suited for the transport of relatively large substances, such as bacteria or dead body cells and is called **phagocytosis** (Figure 3.6), a term that literally means "cell eating." Phagocytosis is routinely conducted by certain white blood cells called *phagocytes*. On the other hand, **pinocytosis** ("cell drinking") is commonly used by cells to take in liquids that contain dissolved proteins or fats.

Exocytosis ("out of a cell") refers to vesicular transport where particles are eliminated from cells (Figure 3.5). Products to be secreted are first packaged into small membrane sacs (vesicles). The sacs migrate to the plasma membrane and fuse with it. This mechanism is often used to secrete hormones, mucus, and other cell products, or to eject certain cellular wastes.

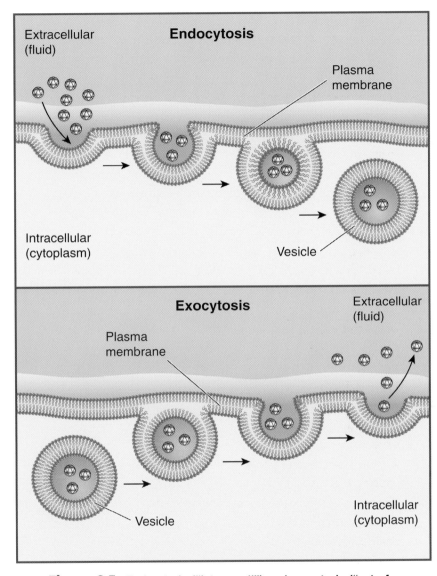

Figure 3.5 Endocytosis ("into a cell") and exocytosis ("out of a cell") are alternate means of moving substances into and out of cells. During the process of endocytosis, the cell membrane surrounds the particles and closes around them, drawing the particles into the cell. The reverse is true for the process of exocytosis. The particles, contained within a vesicle, move to the edge of the cell where the vesicle fuses with the cell membrane and releases the particles.

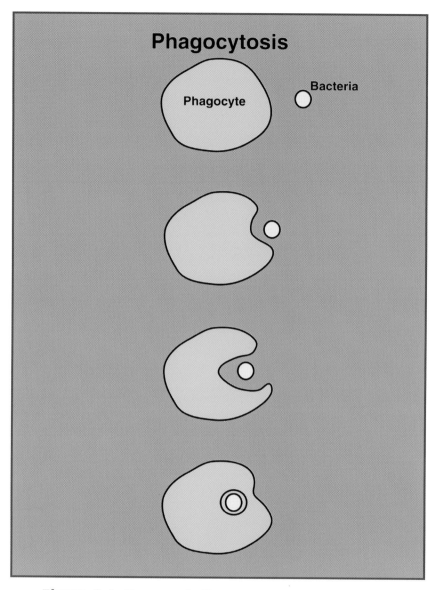

Figure 3.6 Phagocytosis ("cell eating") is a processes used primarily by white blood cells to engulf and destroy bacteria, viruses, or other large foreign particles which could cause harm to the body. The cell, often known as a phagocyte, reaches out "arms" and surrounds the foreign particle, pulling it inside, where various enzymes break down the invader.

CONNECTIONS

Many substances move across membrane surfaces by passive transport, a process that does not require cellular energy. This includes simple diffusion, facilitated diffusion, osmosis, and filtration. In contrast, active transport mechanisms require cellular energy in the form of ATP, such as movement of solutes using pumps or by endocytosis and exocytosis.

Osmosis is a special case of diffusion that occurs when water molecules diffuse from a region of higher water concentration to a region of lower concentration across a selectively permeable membrane. Solutions that have the same osmotic pressure as cells and body fluids are considered isotonic, and they do not cause cells to change size. In contrast, a solution with a higher osmotic pressure than body fluids is hypertonic, and cells placed in this environment will shrink due to the net movement of water out of the cell. Cells exposed to a hypotonic solution, which has a lower osmotic pressure than body fluids, will gain water by osmosis and swell.

4

Cytoplasm:
The Factory and Post Office of Cells

The cellular material located outside the nucleus and inside the plasma membrane is called the **cytoplasm**. It is where most cellular activities take place. In a sense, it could be thought of as a "manufacturing" area of a cell. Not surprisingly, early microscopists using light microscopes thought the cytoplasm was essentially a structureless and functionless gel. This is because the cytoplasm is essentially a clear, colorless substance. However, electron microscopes, which provide much greater magnification and resolution, have revealed that cytoplasm is filled with a rich network of membranes and structures. In fact, the cytoplasm consists of three major components: the *cytosol, organelles,* and *inclusions.* (Refer again to Figure 1.5 on page 21).

COMPONENTS OF THE CYTOPLASM

The **cytosol** is a semitransparent, viscous (thick) fluid in which all the other cytoplasmic elements are suspended. It is mainly composed of water and has nutrients and other solutes dissolved in it.

Inclusions are chemical substances that may or may not be present depending on the cell type. Most inclusions are stored nutrients or cell products. For instance, fat droplets in *adipose* cells and *glycogen* granules in liver cells are both examples of inclusions that store energy. Mucus and pigments, such as **melanin** in skin and hair cells, are inclusions that contain cell products.

Organelles ("little organs") are the structures that actually carry out particular functions for the cell as a whole. Loosely speaking, they are analogous to organs, which carry out complex and specific functions for the entire organism. Some organelles, such as the cytoskeleton, ribosomes, and centrioles, lack cell membranes. However, most organelles are surrounded by a cell membrane, similar in composition and function to the plasma membrane. These include the mitochondria, endoplasmic reticulum, Golgi apparatus, lysosomes, and peroxisomes.

Ribosomes

Ribosomes are tiny, round, non-membranous structures made of proteins and RNA. They are the actual sites of protein synthesis within cells. In a sense, they can be thought of as a zipper, allowing appropriate amino acids to be linked

DID YOU KNOW?

Cell membranes permit organelles to maintain an internal environment different from the surrounding cytosol. In fact, this compartmentalization is absolutely crucial to cell functioning and is arguably the major difference between biology and chemistry. For example, if all the chemicals found in an organelle, such as the mitochondria, were placed *in vitro* (in a test tube), only a small number of appropriate metabolic reactions would occur. This is because cell membranes are necessary for the constituents of an organelle to be appropriately separated or appropriately mixed in order to function as they do *in vivo* (in the living cell). Further, membrane compartmentalization is necessary to prevent the thousands of cellular enzymes and chemicals from randomly mixing, which would cause chaos.

together to form polypeptides. Many ribosomes are found attached to the surface of an organelle called the *endoplasmic reticulum*. They are responsible for making proteins that will be secreted from the cell or incorporated into cell membranes. In contrast, some ribosomes float free within the cytoplasm. They produce soluble proteins that function within the cytosol.

Endoplasmic Reticulum

The **cytomembrane system** refers to a series of organelles (*endoplasmic reticulum*, *Golgi apparatus*, and *vesicles*) that synthesize lipids and also modify new polypeptide chains into complete functional proteins. This system also sorts and ships its products to different locations within the cell.

The cytomembrane system begins with the **endoplasmic reticulum** (ER), a complex organelle composed of membrane-bound, flattened sacs and elongated canals that twist through the cytoplasm. In fact, the ER accounts for about half of the total membrane of a cell. The ER is continuous with the membrane that surrounds the nucleus, and also interconnects and communicates with other organelles. In this capacity, it serves as a micro "circulatory system" for the cell by providing a network of channels that carry substances from one region to another. There are two distinct types of ER: rough ER and smooth ER. The rough ER has many ribosomes attached to its outer surface. This gives it a studded appearance when viewed with an electron microscope. In contrast, smooth ER lacks ribosomes.

Rough ER has several functions. Its ribosomes synthesize all the proteins secreted from cells. Consequently, rough ER is especially abundant in cells that export proteins, such as white blood cells, which make antibodies, and pancreatic cells that produce digestive enzymes. The newly synthesized polypeptides move directly from ribosomes into ER tubules, where they are further processed and modified. For example, sugar groups may be added, forming *glycoproteins.* In addition, proteins may fold into complex, three-dimensional shapes. The rough ER then encloses newly synthesized proteins into vesicles, which pinch off and travel to the *Golgi apparatus.* The rough ER is also responsible for forming the constituents of cell membranes, such as integral proteins and phospholipids.

Smooth ER is continuous with rough ER; however, it does not synthesize proteins. Instead, it manufactures certain lipid molecules, such as *steroid hormones* (i.e., testosterone and estrogen). It is also important for detoxification of some metabolic products and drugs. Because the liver is important for handling toxins, its cells have a well-developed smooth ER. Skeletal muscle cells also have a large amount of smooth ER that is specifically modified to store calcium ions. The release of this calcium, which is stimulated by appropriate nerves, is necessary for muscle contraction to occur.

Golgi Apparatus

The **Golgi apparatus** appears as stacks of flattened membranous sacs (Figure 4.1). Whereas the ER is the "factory" that produces products, the Golgi is a "processing and transportation center." Its enzymes put the finishing touches on newly synthesized proteins and lipids arriving from the rough ER. For example, sugar groups may be added or removed. Phosphate groups also may be attached. The Golgi apparatus then sorts out various products and packages them in vesicles for shipment to specific locations. Thus, like an assembly line, vesicles from the ER fuse with the Golgi apparatus on one side, and newly formed transport vesicles containing the finished product bud off the opposite side. Some of these vesicles may fuse with the plasma membrane for subsequent exocytosis of product. Alternatively, they may fuse with various organelles in the cytoplasm.

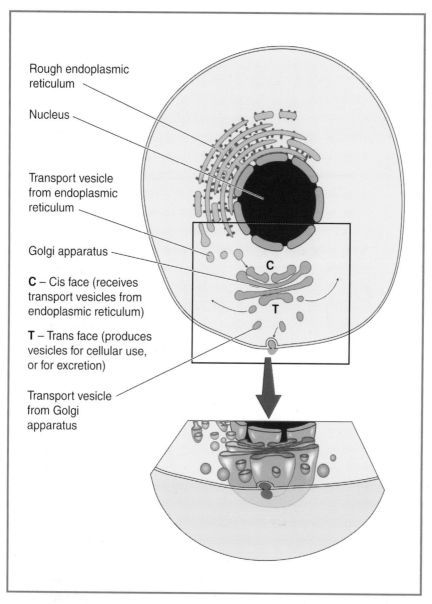

Rough endoplasmic reticulum

Nucleus

Transport vesicle from endoplasmic reticulum

Golgi apparatus

C – Cis face (receives transport vesicles from endoplasmic reticulum)

T – Trans face (produces vesicles for cellular use, or for excretion)

Transport vesicle from Golgi apparatus

Figure 4.1 The Golgi apparatus is the processing and transportation center of the cell. The Golgi receives proteins from the endoplasmic reticulum, adds any necessary finishing touches, and prepares the proteins for delivery to various parts of the cell where they will be used to carry out day-to-day functions.

Vesicles

Vesicles are tiny, membranous sacs found in the cytoplasm. A common type is the **lysosome**, which buds from Golgi membranes. Lysosomes are organelles that contain powerful digestive enzymes that break down nutrient molecules and foreign particles. For instance, certain types of white blood cells engulf bacteria, which are then digested by lysosomal enzymes. Lysosomes also are used to destroy worn out cell parts. In this way, they can be thought of as the "garbage disposal" system of cells.

YOUR HEALTH: Lysosomes

There are several diseases associated with malfunctioning lysosomes. For example, this organelle does not function properly in people with Tay-Sachs disease, an inherited disorder that is most prevalent in Ashkenazi (central European) Jewish children. Those afflicted with this disease lack a single lysosomal enzyme (out of about 40). This, in turn, negatively affects brain cells where this enzyme is important for the continual degradation of certain glycolipids. As a result of this disease, undigested lipids accumulate in nerve cells, interfering with the proper functioning of the nervous system. Affected individuals usually show symptoms of listlessness and motor weakness by 3 to 6 months of age. Soon thereafter mental retardation, seizures, and blindness occur. The disease ultimately leads to death, usually within a year and a half of birth.

Lysosome activity also is important for shrinking or removing particular tissues at certain times during development. For example, lysosome digestion is responsible for removing the webbing between fingers and toes in a human fetus. It also is responsible for degrading a tadpole's tail as the animal develops into an adult frog. In addition, lysosomal digestion of tissue occurs in the uterus after childbirth, the breasts after weaning an infant, and skeletal muscles during periods of prolonged inactivity.

Peroxisomes are tiny sacs of membrane that break down fatty acids and amino acids. They also detoxify a number of poisonous substances. However, the most important function of peroxisomes is the removal of **free radicals**, highly reactive chemicals, such as O_2^-, that are normally produced during cell metabolism. Cigarette smoke and ultraviolet radiation create additional free radicals. Because free radicals lack electrons in their outer shell, they have a powerful ability to oxidize. **Oxidation** refers to the process by which an atom or molecule loses one or more electrons to another atom or molecule, such as to a free radical, thereby disrupting both its structure and ability to function. Oxidation, for instance, is what causes metal to rust. Consequently, excess amount of free radicals can alter essential molecules, such as DNA and enzymes, thereby affecting overall health. In fact, excess free radicals have been implicated with cardiovascular disease, aging, and Alzheimer's disease.

An *antioxidant* is a chemical that gives up an electron to a free radical before it has a chance to damage some other molecule, such as DNA. The body produces some natural antioxidants, including the hormone melatonin, which neutralizes some free radicals. In addition, carotenoids, orange pigments in some vegetables (such as carrots and pumpkins), and foods rich in vitamins C and E provide antioxidant activity. Presently, there is much debate concerning the health benefits and risks of supplementing the diet with antioxidant vitamins.

Mitochondria

Mitochondria are considered the "power plants" of cells because they produce most of its ATP. The metabolic processes that produce ATP in this organelle depend upon a continuous supply of oxygen. They also produce carbon dioxide as a by-product. Mitochondria are particularly abundant in metabolically active cells, such as those in skeletal muscle and liver.

Mitochondria appear as elongated, fluid-filled, sausage-like sacs that vary in size and shape. (Figure 4.2). Their wall consists of two separate cell membranes: a smooth outer membrane and an inner membrane that has a number of large folds called *cristae*, which increases its surface area. Some of the enzymes necessary to make ATP are physically part of the cristae (integral and peripheral membrane proteins). Other enzymes are dissolved in the fluid within the *matrix* (the region enclosed by the inner membrane). Cyanide gas

DID YOU KNOW?

Mitochondria are unusual organelles. In terms of their size and biochemistry, they closely resemble bacteria. In fact, they have their own DNA and ribosomes. However, mitochondrial DNA is circular, like DNA found in bacteria. In addition, mitochondrial ribosomes are more similar to those in bacterial cells than ribosomes in the very cytoplasm that contains mitochondria. Further, the inner membrane of mitochondria closely resembles a bacterial plasma membrane. Mitochondria also are able to reproduce on their own, independent of the cell in which they reside. Taken together, the above evidence is used to support the theory of **endosymbiosis**; *endo-* means within and *symbiosis* means living together. It proposes that over 1.2 billion years ago some forms of free-living bacteria were engulfed by predatory, amoeba-like cells, yet escaped digestion. Over time, these ancient bacteria evolved into modern mitochondria and developed a permanent symbiotic relationship with their host cells.

As mentioned above, mitochondria have the ability to divide on their own. This helps explain how their number may increase in cells undergoing higher levels of metabolic activity. For example, regular exercise will lead to an increase in the number of mitochondria in skeletal muscle. This, in turn, allows the cells of an athlete to produce more ATP than a sedentary person.

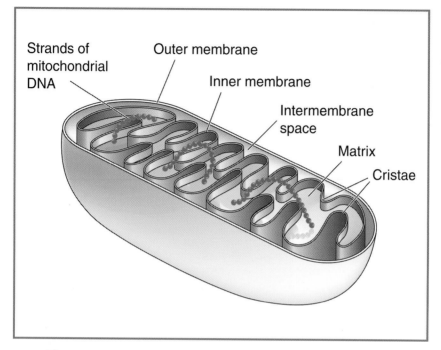

Strands of
mitochondrial
DNA

Outer membrane

Inner membrane

Intermembrane
space

Matrix

Cristae

Figure 4.2 The mitochondria are the cell's energy-producing facilities. They supply the cell with the ATP needed to perform its functions. Mitochondria consist of two separate membranes. The inner membrane has many folds, called cristae, which increase the surface area and thus increase the amount of space where ATP can be produced. The matrix, the innermost portion of the mitochondria, is filled with an enzyme-rich fluid.

is highly toxic because it blocks the production of ATP in mitochondria.

Cytoskeleton

Cells contain an elaborate network of protein structures throughout the cytoplasm called the **cytoskeleton** (Figure 4.3). These structures can be thought of as both the "bones" and "muscles" of cells, because they provide a physical framework that determines cell shape, reinforce the plasma membrane and nuclear envelope, and act as scaffolds for

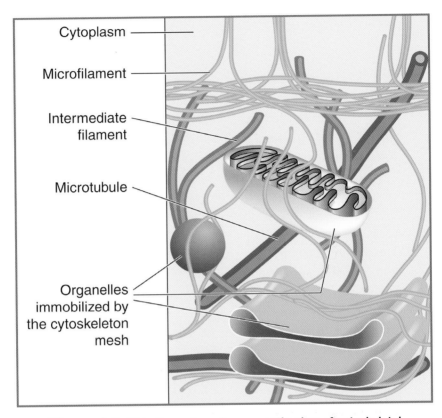

Figure 4.3 This figure is a diagrammatic view of cytoskeletal elements. Microfilaments are strands composed of the protein actin and are involved with cell motility and changes in cell shape. Intermediate filaments are tough protein fibers, constructed like woven ropes, and act as internal wires to resist pulling forces on the cell. Microtubules are hollow tubes made of the protein tubulin. They help determine overall cell shape and the distribution of cellular organelles.

membrane and cytoplasmic proteins. They also are used for intracellular transport and for various types of cell movements. Many of these elements are permanent. However, some only appear at certain times in a cell cycle. For example, before cell division occurs, *spindle fibers* form, which are used to separate **chromosomes** and distribute them to each of the newly formed daughter cells. The spindle fibers then disassemble when cell division is complete. As might be expected, energy from ATP is needed for cytoskeletal movements.

The largest of these structures are **microtubules**, long, hollow cylinders, which help determine overall cell shape. They also act like "railroad tracks," allowing organelles to distribute appropriately within the cytoplasm. In addition, microtubules are vital to cell division, by forming spindle fibers. *Colchicine*, produced by the autumn crocus (*Colchicum*), is a poison that blocks assembly and promotes disassembly of microtubules, affecting animals that eat these plants. This chemical is used in the laboratory to block cell division by scientists that study cell reproduction and cancer. Another plant product, taxol, is a poison from the western yew (*Taxus brevifolia*). It also blocks cell division by disrupting microtubules. Recently, physicians have used taxol to inhibit growth of some tumors, including breast cancer.

The thinnest cytoskeletal elements are **microfilaments**. They are primarily composed of the protein *actin*. Microfilaments are involved with cell motility and in producing changes in cell shape. The most stable of the cytoskeletal elements are the rope-like **intermediate filaments** that mechanically strengthen and help maintain the shape cells and their parts. In some cases, they can be thought of as internal "wires" that resist pulling forces.

Centrioles, Cilia, and Flagella

Centrioles consist of two hollow, non-membranous cylinders that lie at right angles to each other. They are primarily made of microtubules. Centrioles are important in cell reproduction by working with spindle fibers to distribute chromosomes. In some cells, centrioles also may give rise to extensions called **cilia** and **flagella**. Cilia occur in precise patterns and rows on a cell surface, displaying coordinated

Figure 4.4 Cilia, pictured here, help to trap dust and debris and to move particles along. For example, cilia that line the respiratory tract help to prevent smoke and other foreign particles from entering the lungs. They can also help to propel an entire organism, as is the case with certain types of protozoa, whose outer surface is covered with cilia.

beating patterns that produces a wave of motion that sweeps over their surface (Figure 4.4). Ciliated cells line the respiratory tract and are used to move mucus and debris away from the lungs. This ciliary motion is temporarily paralyzed by cigarette smoke, which explains why regular smokers have a chronic cough. Flagella are considerably longer than cilia and display an undulating wavelike motion. The only example of a flagellated cell in the human body is sperm.

CONNECTIONS

The cellular material located outside the nucleus and inside the plasma membrane is called the cytoplasm. It is where most cellular activities take place and consists of three major components: the cytosol, organelles, and inclusions.

Ribosomes are tiny, round, non-membranous structures made of proteins and RNA. They are the sites of protein synthesis within cells. Endoplasmic reticulum (ER) is a complex organelle composed of membrane-bound, flattened sacs and elongated canals that twist through the cytoplasm. Rough ER has many ribosomes attached to its outer surface that synthesize proteins secreted from cells. Rough ER is also responsible for forming the constituents of cell membranes, such as integral proteins and phospholipids. Smooth ER lacks ribosomes and manufactures certain lipid molecules and detoxifies some metabolic toxins. The Golgi apparatus puts the finishing touches on newly synthesized proteins and lipids arriving from the rough ER. It also packages them in vesicles for shipment to specific locations.

Lysosomes are organelles that contain powerful digestive enzymes used to break down nutrients and foreign particles. Peroxisomes are tiny membrane sacs that detoxify a number of poisonous substances and are important in the removal of free radicals. Mitochondria are double-membraned organelles that produce most of a cell's ATP. The endosymbiotic theory suggests they evolved from free-living bacteria. The cytoskeleton is an elaborate network of protein structures in the cytoplasm consisting of microtubules, microfilaments, and intermediate filaments. They provide a physical framework that determines cell shape, reinforce the plasma membrane and nuclear envelope, and act as scaffolds for membrane and cytoplasmic proteins. They also are used for intracellular transport and for various types of cell movements.

5

The Nucleus:
A Command Center for Cells

The nucleus of a cell is a spherical or oval structure averaging about 5 micrometers in diameter, making it the largest cytoplasmic organelle. It is usually located near the center of a cell and is surrounded by a double-layered envelope, consisting of inner and outer lipid bilayer membranes. The nucleus is considered the "command center" of a cell. Its DNA contains the genetic code which has the instructions to produce virtually every protein in the body (recall that mitochondria have their own DNA and produce some proteins not coded for in nuclear DNA). In addition, the nucleus also directs the kinds and amounts of proteins that are synthesized at any given time.

The nucleus has three distinct constituents: the *nuclear*

DID YOU KNOW?

Every cell type in the body contains a nucleus, with one notable exception. Mature red blood cells lose their nucleus before entering the blood stream from bone marrow. As a consequence, these **anucleate** cells cannot synthesize proteins. Therefore, circulating red blood cells do not have the ability to replace enzymes or structural parts that break down. For this reason, they have a limited life span, approximately 3 to 4 months. In contrast, some cells contain many nuclei, such as those in skeletal muscle and the liver. The presence of multiple nuclei usually indicates a relatively large mass of cytoplasm that must be regulated.

envelope, the *nucleolus,* and *chromatin.* These structures are discussed below.

NUCLEAR ENVELOPE

Similar to mitochondria, nuclei are bound by a double-membrane barrier called the **nuclear envelope** (or *nuclear membrane*). It consists of two lipid bilayer membranes in which numerous protein molecules are embedded. This envelope encloses the **nucleoplasm**, the fluid portion of the nucleus. Like the cytoplasm, nucleoplasm contains dissolved salts and nutrients. The outer layer of the nuclear envelope is continuous with rough ER and also is studded with numerous ribosomes. The inner surface has attachment sites for protein filaments that maintain the shape of the nucleus and also anchor DNA molecules, helping to keep them organized.

As with all cell membranes, the nuclear envelope keeps water-soluble substances from moving freely into and out of the nucleus. However, at various points, the two layers of membrane fuse together. **Nuclear pores**, composed of clusters of proteins, are found at such regions and span the entire width of both layers. These pores allow transport of ions and small, water-soluble substances, as well as regulate entry and exit of large particles, such as ribosomal subunits (Figure 5.1).

NUCLEOLI

Each nucleus contains one or more **nucleoli** ("little nuclei"), small, non-membranous, dense bodies composed largely of RNA and protein. Nucleoli are the sites where ribosomal subunits are assembled. Accordingly, they are associated with specific regions of *chromatin* that contains DNA for synthesizing ribosomal RNA. Once ribosomal subunits are formed, they migrate to the cytoplasm through nuclear pores.

CHROMATIN

Chromatin consists of loosely coiled fibers of DNA and *histone* proteins (Figure 5.2). The DNA contains information ("blueprints") for protein synthesis in regions called **genes.**

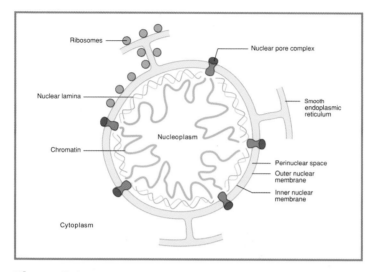

Figure 5.1 The image here is a diagrammatic view of the nuclear envelope, a double-membrane barrier separated by the perinuclear space. The outer nuclear membrane is continuous with the rough ER of the cytoplasm. The inner membrane is lined with a network of protein filaments, the nuclear lamina, that maintain the shape of the nucleus. Note the presence of nuclear pores, a complex of proteins that regulate entry and exit of large particles. The nuclear envelope encloses a gel-like fluid called the nucleoplasm in which other elements are suspended. Chromatin is composed of approximately equal amounts of DNA (our genetic material) and histone proteins, which provide a physical means for packing the very long DNA molecules.

Each gene is a segment of DNA that codes for a specific protein, and it is estimated humans have close to 35,000 different genes. The histone protein molecules associated with chromatin are used to help package a great deal of DNA into a small space. To fully appreciate this task, keep in mind that a nucleus is only about 5 micrometers in diameter. However, the total length of DNA in each nucleus is around 5 centimeters. Thus, in order to pack DNA into a nucleus, there is nearly a 10,000-fold reduction in length! This is accomplished by wrapping DNA around clusters of histone proteins, forming structures that look like beads on a string. In addition, proteins

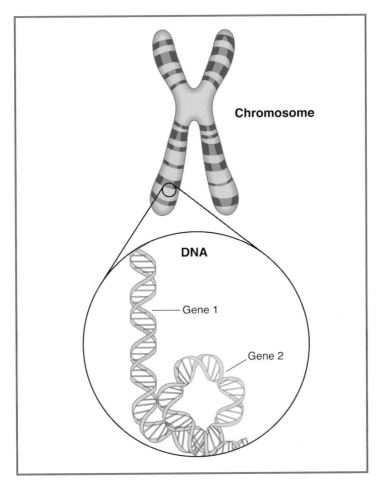

Figure 5.2 DNA is contained within chromosomes, as is shown here. DNA contains the information necessary for protein synthesis in special regions called genes. Scientists estimate that humans have approximately 35,000 different genes which control all aspects of human life from hair color to predisposition to certain diseases.

associated with chromatin provide a regulatory function by helping determine which genes are active.

When a cell is preparing to divide, it duplicates its DNA molecules so each daughter cell will receive all the required hereditary instructions. In addition, prior to cell division, chromatin must be folded and twisted into condensed structures called **chromosomes**. Chromosomes greatly compact the already condensed genetic material in chromatin, preventing entanglement and breakage of delicate strands during the movements that occur during cell division. A chromosome packages genetic material in an analogous way as a skein packages a great length of yarn. In other words, a skein makes it possible for you to transport yarn from the store without it tangling or breaking.

AGING

Aging of individual cells is responsible for many of the problems associated with old age of an organism. Cell aging is a complicated phenomenon that is not completely understood. Some researchers suggest that it results from continual small challenges from toxins, which over time lead to permanent cell damage. For instance, pesticides, alcohol, certain environmental pollutants, and bacterial toxins may damage cell membranes, change the activity of enzymes, and cause mistakes in DNA replication (mutations). In addition, free radicals produced by mitochondria

YOUR HEALTH: Mutations

A **mutation** refers to a change in the structure of DNA. This, in turn, causes a gene to code for one or more inappropriate amino acids, thereby producing an abnormal protein, which may not function properly. A consequence of a mutation can be a specific disease. For example, since most enzymes and many structural components are composed of proteins, mutations can lead to a variety of enzyme deficiency diseases or disorders affecting membrane transport or regulation of metabolism. Sickle cell anemia is an example of an inherited mutation that is caused by an inappropriate substitution of one amino acid in the entire hemoglobin molecule. Mutations also can cause cancer. Excessive exposure to ultraviolet light, X-rays, and some chemicals, such as tars in cigarette smoke, alcohol, and certain environmental pollutants, can cause mutations.

during normal metabolism may damage organelles, which in turn weakens and ages a cell. Free radicals also are generated by exposure to radiation, such as ultraviolet light and X-rays.

Alternatively, other researchers have implicated aging with a progressive weakening of the immune system that occurs as we get older. As a result, the body becomes less able to eliminate damaging infections. In addition, as we age, our immune system becomes more likely to inappropriately attack our own body tissues, leading to their destruction.

Some molecular biologists suggest aging is programmed in our genes. Their evidence comes from the study of **telomeres**, special caps on the end of chromosomes that protect them from fraying or fusing with other chromosomes. By loose analogy, telomeres function similarly as aglets on the end of shoelaces. Telomeres may be related to aging because they shorten slightly after each cell division, and when they reach a certain minimal length, cells stop dividing and die. With this in mind, some searching for a "fountain of youth" suggest the use of chemicals that prevent telomere loss, which in turn may prolong life.

THE CELL CYCLE

The **cell cycle** refers to the series of changes that a cell undergoes from the time it forms until it reproduces. Its stages include *interphase, mitosis, cytoplasmic division*, and *differentiation*. (Figure 5.3)

Interphase describes the period when a cell grows and undergoes its normal metabolic activities. It is usually the longest phase in the cell cycle. In addition, DNA replicates towards the end of interphase as the cell prepares for division.

Many kinds of body cells grow and reproduce, thereby increasing their number, as when a child grows into an adult. In addition, cell division is necessary to replace cells with short life spans, such as those that form skin or the lining of the stomach (which is replaced about every three to five days) or during tissue repair. **Mitosis** refers to division of the nucleus (Figure 5.4).

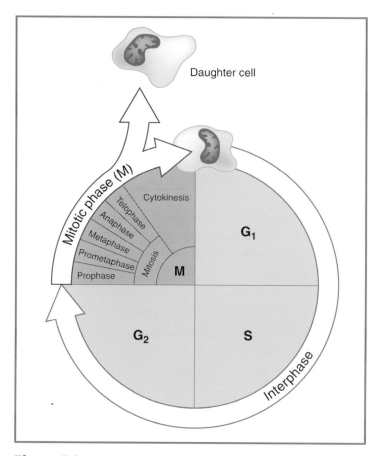

Figure 5.3 A cell undergoes many changes from its formation until the time it reproduces. G_1 and G_2 are growth stages, during which time the cell matures. The chromosomes replicate during the S (synthesis) stage. G_1, G_2, and S are all stages of interphase. During the M (mitotic) phase, the cell undergoes the five stages of mitosis (prophase, prometaphase, metaphase, anaphase, and telophase), as well as cytokinesis, where the two new daughter cells split.

It results in the formation of two daughter nuclei with exactly the same genes as the original cell. Although mitosis is described in terms of phases, it is actually a continuous process. Depending on the type of cell, it may take from 5 minutes to several hours to complete.

The first stage, **prophase**, is characterized by condensation of chromatin into chromosomes. In addition, controls replicate, spindle fibers appear, and the nuclear envelope and nucleoli disappear. Once the nuclear envelope is gone, some of the spindle microtubules attach to chromosomes, throwing them into an agitated motion during prometaphase (also called late prophase). Metaphase describes the stage when chromosomes line up in a straight line midway between the centrioles. This is followed by **anaphase**, when the *chromatids* (two halves of a replicated chromosome) are pulled apart and become individual chromosomes as spindle fibers shorten. Finally, **telophase** is much like prophase in reverse. That is, a nuclear envelope and nucleoli reappear, and the chromosomes unwind, forming threadlike chromatin.

Cytokinesis describes the events that involve division of the cytoplasm. It actually begins during late anaphase, when the cell membrane starts to constrict, and is complete during telophase. Cytokinesis occurs due to contraction of a ring of microfilaments, which forms a **cleavage furrow** over the midline of the spindle, thereby pinching the original mass of cytoplasm into two parts.

All body cells originate from a single cell called the **zygote** (a fertilized egg). However, they do not all look alike or have the same function in an adult organism. This is because cells have the ability to develop different characteristics in a process called **differentiation**. Differentiation is accomplished by individual cells expressing some genes, while simultaneously repressing others. In other words, all the information stored in DNA is not used by every cell. Instead, DNA information required for universal cell processes is active in multiple cell types, whereas information specific to one cell type is only activated in that particular kind of cell.

It should be noted that a different process of cell division is necessary to produce **gametes** (sperm and ova). This is because gametes combine genetic information from two different cells during fertilization to form a zygote. **Meiosis** is a form of nuclear division that occurs in the gonads, which reduces the

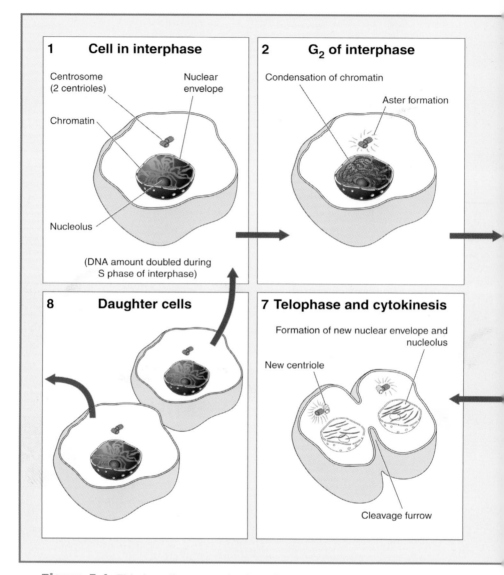

1   Cell in interphase

Centrosome
(2 centrioles)

Nuclear
envelope

Chromatin

Nucleolus

(DNA amount doubled during
S phase of interphase)

2   G$_2$ of interphase

Condensation of chromatin

Aster formation

8   Daughter cells

7 Telophase and cytokinesis

Formation of new nuclear envelope and
nucleolus

New centriole

Cleavage furrow

Figure 5.4 This is a diagrammatic view of the cell cycle. (1) Interphase is a period of cell growth and when a cell carries out its normal functions. (2) The second gap phase (G$_2$) is a relatively brief interval between DNA replication and cell division where a cell completes replication of its centrioles and synthesizes enzymes that control cell division. (3) Chromatin condenses into chromosomes, spindle fibers elongate, and nucleoli and the nuclear envelope disappear during prophase. (4) Some of the spindle fibers attach to chromosomes, causing them to move during prometaphase (also called late prophase). (5) Metaphase is

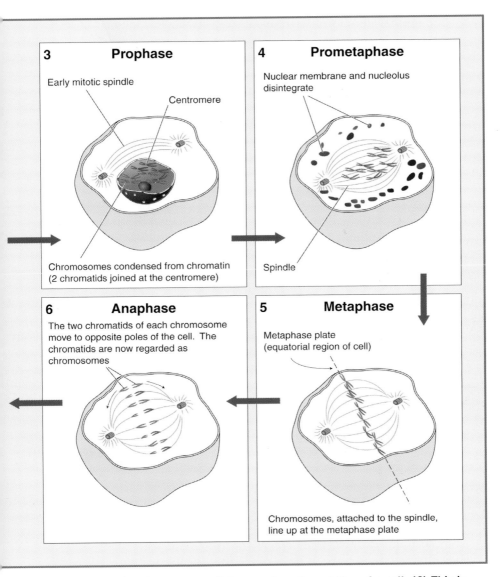

3   Prophase

Early mitotic spindle

Centromere

Chromosomes condensed from chromatin
(2 chromatids joined at the centromere)

4   Prometaphase

Nuclear membrane and nucleolus
disintegrate

Spindle

6   Anaphase

The two chromatids of each chromosome
move to opposite poles of the cell. The
chromatids are now regarded as
chromosomes

5   Metaphase

Metaphase plate
(equatorial region of cell)

Chromosomes, attached to the spindle,
line up at the metaphase plate

characterized by chromosomes lining up along the midline of a cell. (6) This is
followed by anaphase where spindle fibers pull sister chromatids to opposite
poles of a cell. (7) Telophase can be thought of as prophase in reverse; chromatin
decondenses, new nuclear envelope and nucleoli appear, and spindles vanish.
Telophase is the end of nuclear division, but overlaps with cytokinesis, or division
of the cytoplasm (note the formation of cleavage furrows, which pinches the cell
in two). (8) Completion of this cycle results in two daughter cells with identical
sets of genes.

chromosome number of each daughter cell by half. In addition, meiosis consists of two successive divisions of the nucleus, resulting in the production of four daughter cells.

CANCER

Cancer refers to a **malignant** tissue mass that arises from mutations in genes that regulate cell growth and division. In other words, cancer cells do not respond to normal cell-cycle controls, causing them to replicate indefinitely. Cancer is the second leading cause of death in this country, and almost half of all Americans will develop cancer in their lifetime (cardiovascular disease is the number one killer of Americans). The most common forms of cancer originate in the skin, lung, colon, stomach, prostate, breast, and urinary bladder.

Because cancer cells replicate indefinitely, they are considered "immortal." This property results, in part, from the production of telomerase, an enzyme that protects telomeres from degrading with each cell division (telomerase is not found in healthy cells). In addition, cancer cells do not display apoptosis, a mechanism that normally eliminates damaged and unhealthy cells. Further, the altered glycocalyx of cancer cells often prevents them from being recognized and destroyed by cells of the immune system.

A **tumor** is an abnormal cell mass that develops when controls for the cell cycle malfunction. **Benign** tumors tend to grow slowly, although in an unprogrammed way. Because they express cell surface recognition proteins, their cells stick together and therefore rarely *metastasize*. Benign tumors also are surrounded by a capsule, which normally is not penetrated by blood vessels. This, in turn, keeps them from becoming much larger than a few centimeters in diameter. Benign tumors are seldom fatal, with the exception of some brain tumors. Skin moles and warts are both examples of benign tumors

In contrast, **malignant** tumors grow and divide more rapidly. In addition, their cells generally lose their specialized structures and appear *undifferentiated*. For example, cells of malignant tumors often do not construct a normal cytoskeleton. As a result, they become disorganized masses that do not perform normal functions, yet still consume oxygen and produce waste products. Because these cell masses lack capsules, they often are infiltrated with blood vessels, and therefore become quite large. As a result, these tumors can crush vital organs, impede blood flow, and out compete

DID YOU KNOW?

Necrosis is a term that refers to death of a cell, a group of cells, or a region of tissue due to an injury or disease. For instance, necrosis may result from insufficient blood supply because of a hemorrhage (broken blood vessel) or an abnormally large blood clot that blocks the flow through a vessel. Consequently, affected areas will not receive adequate oxygen and nutrients, nor be able to eliminate waste products. Necrosis also may occur from severe trauma or exposure to toxic chemicals and radiation (e.g., infrared, ultraviolet, and X-ray).

In contrast to uncontrolled cell death described by necrosis, sometimes it is necessary for a cell to commit suicide. This process is called **apoptosis**, or *programmed cell death*. It is designed to eliminate cells that are damaged beyond repair or cells that are not needed, excessive in number, or aged. During apoptosis, a series of intracellular enzymes activate in response to damaged molecules within a cell or to an appropriate external signal. The enzymes cut chromatin into many pieces and also destroy the cytoskeleton. As a result, the nuclear envelope breaks down, and the plasma membrane pinches in, causing the cell and its organelles to collapse upon themselves. In this way, damaged cellular contents do not leak out, but instead the cell shrinks and rounds up on itself, making it more easily phagocytized by a white blood cell. Apoptosis also is characteristic of oxygen-starved cells, such as heart cells during a heart attack or brain cells following a stroke.

normal tissues for nutrients. Further, the plasma membranes of malignant tumors do not function properly. For instance, they often do not express *cell adhesion molecules*, which allows cells to break free and enter the blood stream or lymph vessels. This, in turn, allows cancer cells to invade other parts of the body and start growing new tumors, a process called **metastasis** (Figure 5.5).

Agents that cause cancer are called **carcinogens** or **mutagens**. Examples include radiation (X-rays and ultraviolet rays), mechanical trauma, certain viral infections, and many chemicals (including tobacco tars). All these factors have the capability to change DNA, which alters the expression of genes. In some cases, carcinogens convert proto-oncogenes to **oncogenes**. Although proto-oncogenes code for proteins necessary for normal cell division, oncogenes allow cells to become cancerous.

Some normal gene products aid in DNA repair, especially when subtle mistakes occur during DNA replication during interphase. As a result, these genes act as tumor suppressor agents by causing cell division to stop if DNA is damaged beyond repair and then initiating apoptosis. The most well studied **tumor suppressor gene** is the *p53* gene. Unfortunately, tumor suppressor genes can be damaged or altered by carcinogenic agents, which can lead to the formation of malignant tumors. For example, a malfunctioning *p53* gene is linked with some breast cancers. Colon cancer involves both activation of an oncogene, which leads to the formation of a polyp or benign tumor, followed by inactivation of one or more tumor-suppressor genes that cause a malignancy to form.

Whenever possible, surgical removal is recommended for a tumor. However, if surgery is not feasible or metastasis has occurred, radiation or chemotherapy (drugs) is usually prescribed. Both procedures target rapidly dividing cells, with the aim of causing more damage to continuously dividing cancer cells than to healthy cells. However, body tissues that normally

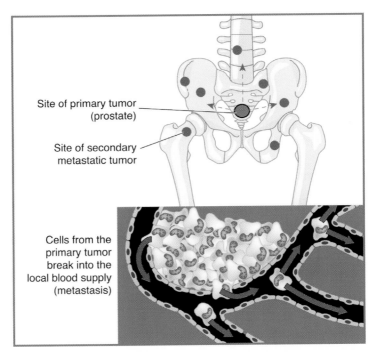

Site of primary tumor
(prostate)

Site of secondary
metastatic tumor

Cells from the
primary tumor
break into the
local blood supply
(metastasis)

Figure 5.5 Cancer cells are cells that grow out of control. The normal checks and balances of the cell cycle, which regulate growth and reproduction, are altered. These cells can remain in their original location and form a tumor (a collection of cells) or metastasize. Metastasis is the process by which cancer cells travel through the body, spreading the disease. A diagram of metastasis is shown here.

have relatively high rates of cell division, such as the lining of the gastro-intestinal tract and hair follicles, also are negatively affected. This explains why nausea, vomiting, and hair loss are common side affects with radiation and chemotherapy.

CONNECTIONS

The nucleus is the largest cytoplasmic organelle and is surrounded by a double-layered envelope, consisting of inner and outer lipid bilayer membranes. It is considered the "command center" of a cell because its DNA contains the genetic code which has the instructions to produce virtually every protein in the body. Each nucleus contains one or more nucleoli, small, non-membranous, dense bodies where ribosomal subunits are assembled. Chromatin consists of loosely coiled fibers of protein and DNA, and contains information for protein synthesis in regions called genes.

The cell cycle refers to the series of changes that a cell undergoes from the time it forms until it reproduces and includes interphase, mitosis, cytoplasmic division, and differentiation. Mitosis is divided into five phases: prophase, prometaphase

A QUESTION TO PONDER:

Stem cells are undifferentiated cells. This property makes them *pluripotent*, meaning they have the potential to differentiate into virtually any cell type found in the body. In fact, the name "stem cell" refers to the notion that all the various cells of the body originate (stem) from them. As you know, every human starts out as a single cell, which has the ability to form all the different cells of the body. As a zygote develops into an embryo, cells begin to differentiate, which depends on activation of some genes and repression of others. As a general rule, once a cell differentiates, it loses the ability to become another cell type.

Some adult tissues, such as the *dermis* of the skin, bone marrow, and brain, contain stem cells. However, because adult stem cells are already somewhat specialized, they do not have the same developmental possibilities as embryonic ones do. Nonetheless, stem cells from adult skin have been successfully induced to form nerve cells.

Embryonic stem cells have several properties that make them more ideal for medicinal use to treat spinal cord injuries or certain diseases, such as Parkinson's disease (degeneration of certain brain cells), Alzheimer's disease (a degenerative brain disorder), diabetes mellitus (a disease of the pancreas affecting blood sugar regulation), and leukemia (a blood cell cancer). In (also known as late prophase), metaphase, anaphase, and telophase. Meiosis is a form of nuclear division that occurs in the gonads, which reduces the chromosome number of each daughter cell by half during the formation of gametes.

A tumor is an abnormal cell mass that develops when controls for the cell cycle malfunction. Benign tumors tend to grow slowly, although in an unprogrammed way, and are generally not fatal. In contrast, malignant tumors grow and divide more rapidly, and their cells appear undifferentiated and are capable of metastasis.

addition to being completely undifferentiated, they grow in culture better than most adult cells. They also induce a less vigorous immune response than adult cells, making tissue rejection less likely.

An ideal source of human stem cells would be those from a very young embryo, typically in the first few days after fertilization. The reason for this is that all the cells at this stage are still undifferentiated and alike. Currently, the only source of embryonic cells is from embryos created in excess of need by fertility clinics for *in vitro* fertilization. However, these are rare and only available to a handful of researchers. Alternatively, the very first tissue in a human fetus suffices for treatment of some diseases, and non-living fetuses are more common than several-day-old embryos as a consequence of legal abortions. Presently, over 100 patients afflicted with Parkinson's disease have received fetal nerve cell transplants.

Not surprisingly, the use of embryonic cells and fetal tissues is highly controversial. Patient advocacy groups recognize potential benefits for treating debilitating illnesses. On the other hand, some human rights groups object to harvesting or using human stem cells under any circumstances. What do you think?

6

Tissues:
When Cells Get Together

Groups of cells that are similar in structure and function are called
tissues. There are four major types of tissues in the human body:
epithelial, connective, muscle, and *nervous,* which are described in
Table 6.1. Tissues have diverse functions in the body, which include
protection, support, transport, movement, storage, and control.
Because organs are made of several tissue types, an understanding of
tissue structure and function will provide an appropriate foundation
for a more thorough understanding of organs and organ systems,
and therefore the human body.

EPITHELIAL TISSUE

Epithelial tissues cover body surfaces, line most internal cavities and
organs, and are the major components of glands. As a boundary
between different environments, epithelial tissues have several different
functions, including protection, absorption (movement of substances
from a cavity into the blood stream), secretion (movement of substances from the blood stream into a cavity), filtration, excretion, and
sensory reception. For example, the epithelium of skin protects underlying tissues from mechanical and chemical damage, and from bacterial
invasion. In contrast, epithelial tissue lining the small intestine is
designed to absorb ingested nutrients, whereas the epithelium of glands
secrete products, such as saliva or digestive enzymes. Some epithelial
tissues in the kidneys are designed to filter blood, and others selectively
absorb and secrete substances in the filtrate in order to produce urine.

Type of Tissue	Location	Function	Special Characteristics
Epithelia	Covers body surfaces, lines internal cavities, and composes glands.	Protection, absorption, secretion, filtration, excretion, and sensory reception.	Avascular, reproduces readily, and cells tightly packed and polarized.
Connective	Widely distributed throughout body.	Binds, supports, protects, fills spaces, stores fat, produces blood cells, and fights infection.	Widely spaced cells, extracellular matrix, and varying degrees of vascularization.
Muscle	Attaches to bones, walls of hollow organs, and the heart.	Allows body movement, propels contents of organs, and pumps blood.	Highly cellular, well vascularized, and contractile.
Nervous	Brain, spinal cord, and peripheral nerves.	Coordinates, regulates, and integrates body functions. Sensory reception and perception.	Neurons conduct electrical impulses, and neuroglia insulate and nourish neurons.

Table 6.1 Groups of cells which work together for a common goal are called tissues. The human body has four major types of tissues. These tissues, their locations, functions, and special characteristics are listed in this table. Note that while some tissues have common functions, all are necessary to sustain life.

Epithelial tissues have several unique characteristics. As a general rule, they are *avascular*, meaning they lack blood vessels. They therefore obtain necessary substances by diffusion from blood vessels located in underlying connective tissues. Epithelial cells have the capacity to reproduce readily. For instance, the inner lining of the small intestine is replaced about every five days. In addition, injuries to an epithelium heal quickly as new cells replace lost or damaged ones. This explains in part how an abrasion or cut in the skin heals. Epithelial cells are also tightly packed, with little intercellular space and material between them. In fact, adjacent cells are usually bound together at many points by special contacts found in the plasma membrane. It is this tight packing of cells that makes epithelia effective barriers.

Finally, because epithelia cover surfaces, they always have one free side; that is, a side exposed to the outside of the body or an internal cavity. This exposed side is called the **apical surface.** The opposite side, or **basal surface,** is anchored to underlying tissues by a non-living substance called the **basement membrane.** Interestingly, the two cell surfaces (apical and basal) have different properties, resulting from different peripheral and integral proteins in their membranes. As a result, cells with distinct basal and apical surfaces are said to be **polarized.** It also is common for the apical surface of epithelial cells to possess **microvilli,** finger-like extensions of the plasma membrane that tremendously increase surface area.

The basement membrane located underneath the basal surface is actually composed of two distinct layers. Its outer layer, the **basal lamina,** is secreted by epithelial cells, whereas the inner **reticular lamina** is made by cells of the underlying connective tissue. Together these two layers provide support and attachment for epithelial tissues (Figure 6.1).

Types of Epithelial Tissue

Epithelial tissues are classified according to the shape of their cells. Flat, scale-like cells are called **squamous,** whereas cube-shaped cells are considered **cuboidal.** Cells that are shaped like a column or cylinder are termed **columnar. Transitional** cells change their shape as the particular tissue they are located in stretches. Epithelia also are classified according to the number of cell layers they contain. For instance, epithelia composed of a single layer of cells are considered **simple,** whereas those made of multiple layers are called **stratified.** However, sometimes a single layer of cells can appear multi-layered because some of the cells do not extend all the way to the apical surface. This arrangement describes **pseudostratified** epithelia. (Figure 6.2).

Simple squamous epithelium consists of a single layer

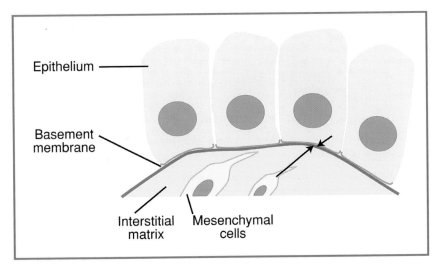

Figure 6.1 This figure is a diagrammatic view of the basement membrane, an extracellular layer that defines an epithelial boundary and also helps reinforce epithelial sheets, resisting stretching and tearing. The basement membrane is actually two layers. The outer layer, the basal lamina, is secreted by epithelial cells, whereas the reticular lamina is formed by underlying connective tissue (indicated by the two arrows). Mesenchymal cells are found in an embryo and are the source of all connective tissues, which secrete an interstitial (extracellular) matrix that contains ground substance and protein fibers.

of flattened, scale-like cells, which allow substances to easily pass through. That is why this tissue type is a common site for diffusion and filtration. For instance, simple squamous epithelia lines the air sacs (alveoli) of the lungs and also the inside walls of blood capillaries. Simple cuboidal epithelium forms a single layer of cube-shaped cells. It covers structures in the ovaries and lines tubules within the kidneys and many glands, such as salivary glands, the thyroid gland, and the pancreas. Simple columnar epithelium is a single layer of elongated cells and is found in the uterus and most organs of the digestive tract, including the stomach and small intestine.

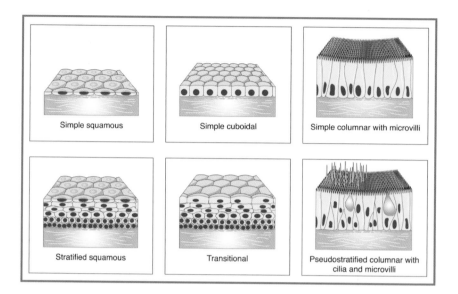

Simple squamous

Simple cuboidal

Simple columnar with microvilli

Stratified squamous

Transitional

Pseudostratified columnar with cilia and microvilli

Figure 6.2 Epithelial tissues are classified according to both the shape of their cells and the number of cells they contain. Squamous cells are flat, cuboidal cells are cube-shaped, and columnar cells are shaped like a column or cylinder. The tissues can also have a single layer of cells (simple), or several layers (stratified). Pseudostratified epithelium has a single layer of cells, but appears stratified because some of the cells do not extend all the way through the tissue.

Pseudostratified columnar epithelium appears stratified or layered, but is not (although all of the cells are anchored to the basement membrane, not all of them reach the apical surface, giving the tissue a multilayerd appearance). These cells line the respiratory passages and reproductive systems, and are often ciliated. In the respiratory system, their cilia move mucus and trapped particles, such as dust and microorganisms, away from the lungs. Stratified squamous epithelium contains several layers of cells, with those in the outermost layers being squamous. However, cells in the deeper layers may be more cuboidal or columnar in shape. This type of tissue lines surfaces of the mouth, throat, vagina, and anal canal. It also forms the outer layer of the skin (the epidermis). Finally, transitional epithelium consists of several layers of cells, which vary in appearance from cuboidal to squamous depending on the degree to which the tissue is stretched. This tissue type is found in the urinary bladder and parts of the uterus and urethra.

Epithelia also form secretory parts of glands, structures that are specialized to produce and release specific substances. Glands that secrete their products into ducts opening onto external surfaces or into internal body cavities are called **exocrine glands**. Examples of exocrine glands include salivary glands, sweat glands, pancreatic glands, mammary glands, and sebaceous glands. In contrast, glands that secrete their products (*hormones*) into tissue fluids or the blood stream are called **endocrine glands**. These include the thyroid gland, adrenal glands, and pituitary gland (Figure 6.3).

CONNECTIVE TISSUE

Connective tissues are the most widely distributed and abundant of the four tissue types. They also have numerous and varied functions, which include binding structures, providing support and protection, serving as a framework, filling spaces, storing fat, producing blood cells, protecting against infection, and helping repair tissue damage. Connective tissues also vary widely regarding their degree of vascularization. Cartilage, for example, is essentially avascular, and ligaments and tendons are poorly vascularized. In contrast, bone is vascularized, and adipose tissue has a rich supply of blood vessels.

Although connective tissues display a tremendous amount of morphological and functional diversity, they all share some common properties. For example, all connective tissues have a common embryological origin. In addition, they are all surrounded by a non-living **extracellular matrix**, secreted by the connective tissue cells. Thus, unlike all other primary tissue types that are composed mostly of cells,

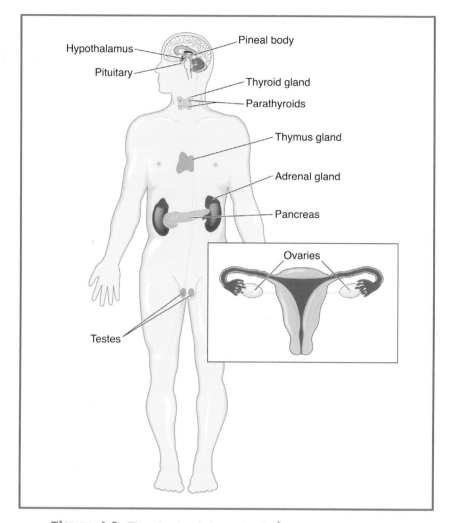

Figure 6.3 The glands of the endocrine system, pictured here, are composed of epithelial tissue. Specifically, the epithelial cells compose the secretory parts of the glands, allowing them to secrete their products (hormones) throughout the body.

connective tissues are largely composed of nonliving matrix, which may widely separate living cells. However, it is this matrix that provides most connective tissues with the ability to withstand great tension and physical trauma.

The extracellular matrix is composed of protein *fibers* and *ground substance*. The fibers provide physical support. The strongest and most common type of fiber is composed of **collagen**. Collagen fibers are found in structures that resist pulling forces, such as tendons, which are used to connect muscles to bones. **Elastic fibers** are composed of the protein **elastin**. They have a greater ability to stretch than collagen fibers, and also have a great tolerance to repeated bending. **Elastic cartilage** is found in the external ear, vocal cords, and epiglottis (the flap that prevents food from entering the respiratory passages). In contrast, **ground substance** serves as connective tissue "glue," filling the space between cells and containing protein fibers. Depending on the type of connective tissue, ground substance can be liquid (blood), semisolid or gel-like (cartilage), or very hard (bone).

Types of Connective Tissue

Bone is the most rigid connective tissue. Its living cells, called **osteocytes**, reside in cavities called **lacunae**. The lacunae are surrounded by an extracellular matrix deposited in layers arranged in concentric circles known as *lamellae*, which together form the basic structural unit of bone called an **osteon.** Many osteons glued together form a large part of the substance of bone. The hardness of bone is due to mineral salts deposited in the extracellular matrix. The matrix also contains a significant amount of collagen, which keeps the bone from becoming brittle (without collagen, bone would have a consistency similar to chalk. On the other hand, with only collagen, bone would be more like a garden hose). Bone is used to support body structures, protect vital organs (skull and ribs), provide attachment sites for muscles, and store minerals, such as calcium and phosphate. In addition, bone marrow produces blood cells.

Cartilage is a flexible tissue, consisting of cells called **chondrocytes** that also sit within lacunae. There are three types of cartilage. The most abundant is **hyaline cartilage**, which is designed to provide support and flexibility. For instance, it is used to attach ribs to the breastbone (*sternum*), form the voice box (*larynx*), and cover the ends of bones where they form joints. It also is found in the soft part of the nose. **Elastic cartilage** is more flexible than hyaline cartilage, and is found in the external ear. **Fibrocartilage** forms cushion-like disks between the vertebrae of the backbone and also between bones in the knee joint.

Dense connective tissue contains many tightly woven fibers of collagen, which are produced by **fibroblasts**. It is found in structures that are designed to act as strapping material, such as *tendons* and *ligaments* (structures that connect bone to bone). It also makes up the **dermis**, the lower layers of skin. The fibroblasts that compose dense (and loose) connective tissue also help repair tears in body tissues. For example, when skin is cut, fibroblasts move to the area of the wound and produce collagen fibers that help close the wound and provide a surface upon which the outer layer of skin can grow.

Loose connective tissues have more cells and fewer fibers than any other type of connective tissue, except for blood. The most widely distributed loose connective tissue is **areolar tissue**. It forms delicate, thin membranes throughout the body and acts as a packing material and glue. For example, it binds skin to underlying organs and also fills spaces between muscles. In addition, it wraps small blood vessels and nerves. Because of the loose and fluid nature of its extracellular matrix, it provides a reservoir of water and salts for surrounding tissues. In fact, virtually all body cells obtain nutrients from the matrix of areolar tissue (and they also release waste products into it). When a body region becomes inflamed, such as from an infection, areolar tissue takes up excess fluid like a sponge, causing the area to swell (a condition called *edema*).

Adipose tissue is a type of loose connective tissue that is designed to store fat in droplets within the cytoplasm of its cells. It helps forms the tissue layer beneath skin (**subcutaneous layer**), where it insulates the body from temperature changes. Adipose tissue also cushions and protects some organs, such as the kidneys, heart, and eyeballs. In addition, adipose stores fat in the abdominal membranes and hips as an energy reserve.

Blood is a special connective tissue consisting of a liquid matrix called **plasma**. In this case, the fibers of the extracellular matrix are soluble proteins in the plasma that become visible during blood clotting. Blood is mainly designed to transport substances within the body, including nutrients from digested food, waste products, respiratory gases, hormones, and antibodies. In addition, blood flow also can be used for temperature regulation by distributing heat throughout the body and also to the skin surface when it is necessary to dissipate heat to the external environment.

DID YOU KNOW?

Cartilage is avascular, and tendons and ligaments are poorly vascularized. In addition, older chondrocytes lose their ability to divide. This explains why these three types of connective tissues heal very slowly when injured. In addition, later in life cartilage tends to calcify, making its matrix resemble that of bone, and its ability to heal virtually impossible.

Adipose tissue can be used to cushion certain organs, helping hold them in place. This function becomes readily apparent in individuals who are severely malnourished and emaciated, as can happen with the eating disorder *anorexia nervosa*. If there is insufficient dietary intake of calories, the fatty encasement around the kidneys can diminish, which may cause the organs to lower their position. This, in turn, can kink the ureters, blocking urine flow to the bladder. As a result, urine backs up into the kidneys, causing severe damage and ultimately renal failure.

Erythrocytes (red blood cells) function in transporting oxygen to cells and also in carrying some carbon dioxide away. **Leukocytes** (white blood cells) are responsible for fighting infections, whereas **platelets** are involved with blood clotting.

Blood also plays an important role in temperature regulation. This is accomplished in part by altering its flow patterns, which occurs by changing the diameter of vessels. **Vasodilation** refers to increasing the diameter of blood vessels, which increases blood flow. Vasodilation of vessels under the skin surface occurs when it is necessary to release heat to the external environment. This explains why skin looks flushed when someone is overheated. In contrast, **vasoconstriction** of skin blood vessels conserves body heat by restricting blood flow to deep body areas, virtually by-passing skin. Because skin is separated from deeper organs by an insulating layer of adipose tissue, heat loss through the outer layer is reduced in this case. Restricting blood flow to the skin for short periods of time does not pose a problem. However, restriction of blood flow for extended periods of time can lead to frostbite. This is because the temperature of the outer body layer approaches that of the external environment, which can cause skin to freeze. In addition, skin cells die if they are deprived of oxygen and nutrients for too long.

MUSCLE TISSUE

Muscle tissues are highly cellular, well vascularized, and have the ability to generate force by contracting. There are three different types of muscle tissue: **skeletal**, **smooth**, and **cardiac** (Figure 6.4). *Skeletal muscle* is attached to bones and is consciously controlled. Under a microscope, its cells are cylindrical in shape, and reveal alternating light and dark patterns called *striations* (that is why this tissue type is sometimes called *striated muscle*). Skeletal muscle is responsible for generating movements of the limbs, trunk,

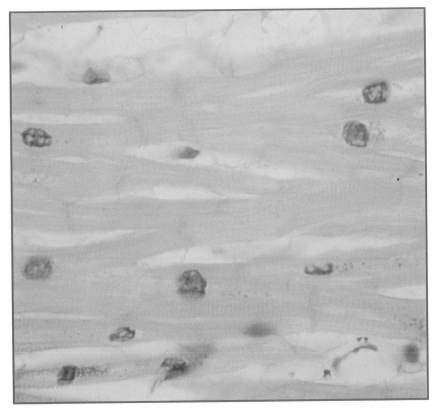

Figure 6.4 Muscle is a type of connective tissue. Skeletal muscle cells are striated and may have multiple nuclei, as can be seen in the picture here. Multiple nuclei are important for muscle cells that are very large or must control a lot of movement.

and head, as well as allowing us to make facial expressions, talk, chew, swallow, breathe, and write. In addition, skeletal muscle helps maintain posture, stabilizes joints, and generates heat (*shivering* refers to involuntary contractions of skeletal muscle).

The cells of *smooth muscle* lack striations, and this tissue type is considered involuntary. However, disciplined individuals who practice yoga or *biofeedback* can develop the ability to control some smooth muscle action. Smooth muscle is found in the walls of blood vessels (except capillaries) and the airways (*bronchioles*), where its contraction reduces flow of blood or air, respectively. Smooth muscle also is located in the walls of hollow organs, such as the stomach, intestines, uterus, and urinary bladder, where it aids in propelling contents.

Cardiac muscle is only found in the walls of the heart. Its contractions are responsible for pumping blood. Like skeletal muscle, its cells have a striated appearance when observed with a microscope. However, similar to smooth muscle, the contractions of this tissue are generally considered involuntary. A unique anatomical property of cardiac muscle is a specialized junction that electrically connects heart cells, thereby allowing a rapid conduction of impulses throughout the heart muscle. This junction is called an *intercalated disk*.

NERVOUS TISSUE

Nervous tissue makes up the brain, spinal cord, and peripheral nerves, which coordinate, regulate, and integrate many body functions. Nervous tissue consists of two major cell types: *neurons* and *neuroglia*. **Neurons** are the cells that generate and conduct electrical impulses, sometimes over substantial distances. These impulses influence other neurons, muscles, and glands. Some neurons have the ability to convert external stimuli, such as light, heat, or sound, into electrical signals that can be recognized by the brain. Most neurons have a *cell body*, which contains a nucleus and most organelles. *Dendrites* are highly branched processes of the cell body that are designed to receive information. Impulses are carried away from the cell body by a single, long process called an *axon* (Figure 6.5).

Neuroglia do not generate and conduct nerve impulses as do neurons. However, they are essential for normal neuronal function. Some neuroglia wrap themselves repeatedly around an axon, forming layers of membrane called a **myelin sheath**. This sheath acts as electrical insulation, which increases the rate at which impulses are conducted (over 100 meters per

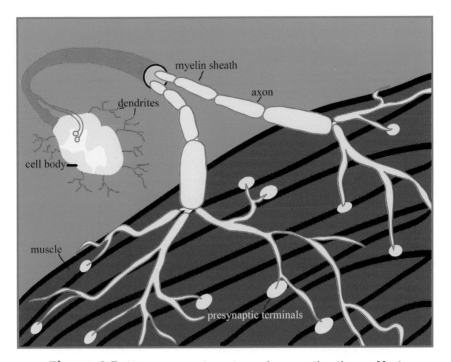

Figure 6.5 Neurons are also a type of connective tissue. Most neurons contain dendrites, which receive the electrical impulse, a cell body, which processes the impulse, and an axon, which transmits the impulse to another cell. The axon may be covered by the myelin sheath, which insulates the axon to increase impulse transmission. The neuron in this diagram is carrying a signal to a muscle cell.

second for some neurons). Other neuroglial cells are phagocytic, whereas some provide neurons with nutrients by connecting them to blood vessels.

CONNECTIONS

Groups of cells that are similar in structure and function are called tissues. There are four major types of tissues in the human body: epithelial, connective, muscle, and nervous. Tissues have diverse functions, which include protection, support, transport, movement, storage, and control.

Epithelial tissues cover body surfaces, line most internal cavities and organs, and are the major component of glands. As a boundary between different environments, epithelial tissues have several different functions, including protection, absorption, secretion, filtration, excretion, and sensory reception.

Connective tissues are the most widely distributed and abundant of the four tissue types. They also have numerous

YOUR HEALTH: Multiple Sclerosis

The importance of neuroglia to nerve transmission becomes evident when studying the disease multiple sclerosis (MS), a chronic, progressive, degenerative disorder that affects nerve fibers in the central nervous system. This disease is the most common neurological cause of debilitation in young people, with an average age of onset between 18 and 35 years. It affects 500,000 people in the United States and is more common in women and in Caucasians. MS is classified as an *autoimmune disease*, which means the immune system inappropriately attacks "self-cells." This immune response is apparently triggered by genetic, environmental, and/or viral factors. In the particular case of MS, the neuroglial cells that wrap around axons in the central nervous system are attacked. This, in turn, leads to progressive destruction of the myelin sheaths. As a result, there is substantial short-circuiting of electrical signals and eventually impulse conduction ceases. Symptoms vary depending on the specific nerve fibers that are affected, but include reduced vision, muscle weakness, clumsiness, and urinary incontinence. Interestingly, neuronal axons are not damaged and may even show some recovery by increasing their number of ion channels. This apparently accounts for periods of *remission* (temporary recovery). However, these are typically followed by further cycles of relapse, as additional myelin is destroyed. Eventually blindness and paralysis may occur.

and varied functions, which include binding structures, providing support and protection, serving as a framework, filling spaces, storing fat, producing blood cells, protecting against infection, and helping repair tissue damage. In addition, they are surrounded by a non-living extracellular matrix, which is secreted by connective tissue cells. Examples of connective tissue includes, bone, cartilage, dense connective tissue (tendons and ligaments), loose connective tissue (areolar and adipose), and blood.

Muscle tissues are highly cellular, well vascularized, and have the ability to generate force by contracting. There are three different types of muscle tissue: skeletal, smooth, and cardiac. Nervous tissue makes up the brain, spinal cord, and peripheral nerves, which coordinate, regulate, and integrate many body functions. Nervous tissue consists of two major cell types: neurons (the cells that generate and conduct electrical impulses) and supporting neuroglia.

7

Skin:
An Exemplary Organ

Two or more tissue types may be organized into more complex structures called **organs,** which perform specific functions for the body. Many organs, such as skin, are composed of all four tissue types. Although skin is often referred to as the **cutaneous membrane**, it is by definition an organ. In fact, skin, is one of the largest organs of the body. In an average adult, it weighs 4−5 kilograms (9−11 pounds), accounting for about 7% of total body weight. Along with its derivatives (sweat glands, oil glands, hair, and nails) and accessory structures (blood vessels and nerves) skin is part of the **integumentary system** (the word integument refers to a covering).

FUNCTIONS OF SKIN

Skin is absolutely essential for **homeostasis**, the ability to maintain a relatively constant environment within the body. A primary function of skin is forming a barrier that protects the body from dehydration. In fact, the biggest threat to survival for terrestrial animals is dehydration, and the waterproof nature of skin keeps fluids and other important substances inside. Skin also protects the entire body from mechanical injury (bumps, abrasions, and cuts), as well as chemical damage (acids and bases). In addition, skin shields us from continual bacterial invasion and ultraviolet radiation in sunlight.

The skin plays an important role in temperature regulation.

This is accomplished with its rich blood supply and sweat glands, which are controlled by the nervous system. For example, during strenuous exercise, excess heat may be eliminated through dilated surface blood vessels and by activating sweat glands. Because sweat contains water, salts, and urea, the integumentary system technically has an excretory function.

Skin also synthesizes vitamin D from modified cholesterol molecules when exposed to ultraviolet radiation (actually vitamin D is not a true vitamin because individuals with adequate exposure to sunlight do not require dietary supplementation). Vitamin D is necessary for the small intestine to absorb dietary calcium. That is why a lack of this vitamin can lead to the disease *rickets*, a disorder characterized by inadequate mineralization of bones. Symptoms include bowed legs and deformities of the pelvis, skull, and rib cage. Finally, skin contains components of the nervous system that detect temperature, touch, pressure, and pain stimuli. As a

DID YOU KNOW?

Arguably, *homeostasis* is the single most important concept of physiology, a branch of biology that deals with the functions and vital processes of living organisms or their parts. In fact, the concept of homeostasis is used as a central *paradigm* (model) to explain the complex processes of animal physiology. During the late nineteenth century, the French physiologist Claude Bernard wrote "all the vital mechanisms, however varied they may be, have only one object, that of preserving constant the condition of life in the inner environment." In the early twentieth century, the American physiologist Walter Cannon coined the word homeostasis ("stable condition") to describe Bernard's concept of the inner environment. Thinking in terms of homeostasis provides a clearer understanding of how and why the human body functions the way it does. In other words, all the cells, tissues, organs, and systems are designed to work together to maintain a relatively constant internal environment.

result, skin provides us with a great deal of information about our external environment.

STRUCTURE OF SKIN

Skin has two tissue layers: the *epidermis* and *dermis* (Figure 7.1). The outer **epidermis** is composed of stratified squamous epithelium. In contrast, the thicker **dermis** is made of connective tissue. As is true for all epithelial tissues, blood vessels are absent in the epidermis (i.e., it is *avascular*), but present in the dermis. Although the two skin layers are firmly connected, a burn or friction can cause them to separate, forming a *blister*.

The skin's **subcutaneous tissue** or *hypodermis* is technically not part of skin. However, it shares many of the skin's protective functions. The hypodermis consists mostly of adipose tissue and some areolar connective tissue. It helps anchor skin, stores fat, and acts as thermal and mechanical insulation. Because of its extensive adipose, hypodermis can thicken when one gains weight, which occurs in a gender-specific manner in adults. For instance, females tend to accumulate excess fat in the thighs, hips, and breasts, whereas men first increase adipose in the abdomen.

Epidermis

The epidermis is composed of four different cell types and is organized into four or five layers called *strata*. The most abundant cell type is the **keratinocyte**. It produces a fibrous protein called **keratin** that gives the epidermis its protective properties. Keratinocytes arise in the deepest layer of the epidermis by mitosis and are gradually pushed outwards towards the skin surface. During this migration, these cells flatten, fill with keratin, and die. That means the outer layer of skin is actually composed of dead cells, and millions of dead keratinocytes are rubbed off every day (it has been estimated that we lose about 40 pounds of skin cells in an

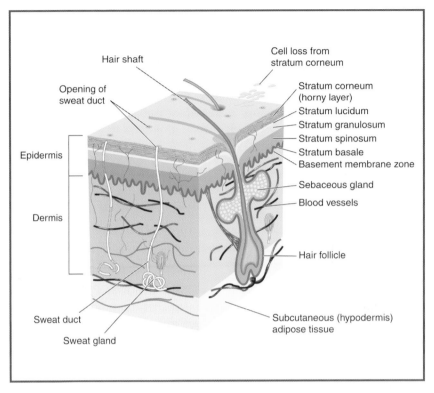

Hair shaft

Opening of
sweat duct

Cell loss from
stratum corneum

Stratum corneum
(horny layer)
Stratum lucidum
Stratum granulosum
Stratum spinosum
Stratum basale
Basement membrane zone

Sebaceous gland

Blood vessels

Hair follicle

Epidermis

Dermis

Sweat duct

Sweat gland

Subcutaneous (hypodermis)
adipose tissue

Figure 7.1 The skin is made up of two layers, the epidermis and the dermis. The outer layer, the epidermis, is composed of stratified squamous epithelial cells. The dermis, which resides below the epidermis, is composed of connective tissue. The diagram here displays a cross section human skin, detailing the epidermis and dermis as well as many components of each layer.

average lifetime). The total life span of a keratinocyte, from its formation to being rubbed off, is 25 to 45 days. In addition, persistent friction can increase the rate of cell production and keratin formation, leading to a thickening of the epidermis called a *callus.*

Melanocytes are cells located near the base of the epidermis. They produce a pigment called **melanin**, which influences skin color and also absorbs ultraviolet radiation.

Melanin is released from melanocytes and then transferred to keratinocytes, where it accumulates over the nucleus forming a "pigment shield." **Langerhan's cells** belong to a group of cells called *macrophages* (white blood cells capable of phagocytosis). They originate in bone marrow and migrate to the epidermis, where they recognize and ingest foreign substances, such as bacteria. In this regard, they play a role in immunity. Finally, **Merkel cells**, present at the epidermal-dermal junction, are associated with sensory nerve endings, forming a *Merkel disk*. These structures function as sensory receptors for touch.

The deepest epidermal layer is the **stratum basale**, which is firmly attached to the dermis. It mainly consists of a single row of cuboidal-shaped cells capable of rapid cell division. About one-fifth of the cells in this layer are melanocytes. There is also an occasional Merkel cell in this stratum. Sometimes invasion by a *papilloma virus* causes a dramatic increase in the rate of cell division. This, in turn, causes a wart to form, which is a type of *benign tumor.*

The next layer is the **stratum spinosum** ("spiny layer"). It contains several layers of cuboidal cells, with scattered melanin granules and Langerhan's cells. The **stratum granulosum** ("granular layer") consists of three to five layers of flattened cells containing *keratohyalin,* a substance that contributes to the formation of keratin. It turns out all the cells above this layer die because they are too far from dermal capillaries to obtain adequate nutrients.

The **stratum lucidum** ("clear layer") contains three to four layers of flattened dead cells. This layer is only found in the palms of the hands and soles of the feet, areas known as "thick skin." The outermost layer is the **stratum corneum** ("horny layer"). It consists of 20 to 30 rows of flat, dead cells completely filled with keratin. It is this layer that prevents water loss and protects from us from biological, chemical, and physical insults. Dandruff occurs when dry patches of epidermal cells flake off the scalp. This affliction is most common in middle age, and also is associated with stress and a high fat diet.

Dermis

The dermis lies below the epidermis, and it corresponds to animal hides used to make leather products. Unlike the epidermal layer, it does not wear away. This explains why tattoos, ink droplets injected into the dermal layer, are relatively permanent. The dermis also differs from the epidermis in that it contains nerves, sensory receptors, blood vessels, hair follicles, oil glands, and sweat glands.

The dermis has two layers. The thinner outer **papillary layer** consists of loose (areolar) connective tissue with collagen and elastic fibers. Its outer surface forms obvious folds, called *dermal papillae.* Many of these papillae contain receptors for touch and pain. In addition, these folds reach up to the epidermis, causing ridges on the surface of skin that increase friction, thereby enhancing the gripping ability of hands and feet. The specific patterns of papillary folds are genetically determined. Because the ridges on the fingertips have a rich supply of sweat pores, they may leave unique *fingerprints,* essentially outlines of sweat on the surfaces they touch.

YOUR HEALTH: Scars

Scars often form following a break in skin. It turns out that scars do not develop when an injury is confined to the epidermis. However, when damage or surgical incision penetrates into the dermis, scar tissue can appear. It results from collagen-producing cells increasing their activity in response to tissue damage. In turn, the newly produced material is pushed to the skin surface. Consequently, scar tissue lacks an epidermal layer. Therefore, when compared to normal skin, it usually has denser collagen fibers, fewer blood vessels, and no hair.

The deeper and thicker **reticular layer** is composed of dense connective tissue. It contains a combination of collagen and elastic fibers in the extracellular matrix, which allows skin to stretch and then return to its original shape. However, substantial body weight gain, as with pregnancy or obesity, can tear the dermis, resulting in visible lines called *stretch marks*. Also, the resilience of skin decreases with age, as collagen fibers stiffen and elastic fibers lose their elasticity. These effects, along with a reduction in the ability of the dermis to hold moisture, produce wrinkles and sagging skin, which usually first become apparent by the late forties. The reticular layer also contains blood vessels, sweat and oil glands, and receptors for the sensation of deep pressure.

SKIN COLOR

Two main factors contribute to skin color: the quantity and distribution of pigments (melanin and carotene) in the skin, and blood flow. Melanin is a skin pigment made of amino acids. It comes in two forms: yellow to red (*pheomelanin*) and the more common brown to black (*eumelanin*). Although melanin is only produced by melanocytes, it is continually released by exocytosis from these cells. Surrounding cells subsequently accumulate the pigment by endocytosis. Interestingly, all people have roughly the same number of melanocytes. That means variations in skin color are due to differences in the form and amount of melanin produced, and in the way it is dispersed. (Figure 7.2)

The most important factor in determining melanin production is a person's genetic predisposition: that is, the particular characteristics inherited from the parents. Also, melanocytes are stimulated by exposure of skin to sunlight, causing them to increase their production of melanin. This response helps protect DNA when there is an increased exposure to ultraviolet radiation. It also is responsible for the development of a tan. However, excessive exposure to

Figure 7.2 Skin color is determined by a pigment called melanin. Melanin is produced by special cells called melanocytes and distributed to other cells throughout the body. A person with more melanin in his or her body will have a darker skin color.

sunlight causes clumping of elastic fibers, which leads to wrinkles and leathery-looking skin. More importantly, excessive exposure to ultraviolet light temporarily suppresses the immune system and also can alter DNA enough to cause skin cancer (described in further detail in Chapter 9). The protective nature of melanin is illustrated by the observation that black people seldom have skin cancer, whereas this disease is much more common in fair-skinned individuals. Freckles and moles are local accumulations of melanin. **Albinism** is an inherited disorder in which melanocytes are incapable of producing melanin.

Carotene is a yellow-orange pigment that can influence skin color. It is found in many food items, such as carrots, apricots, and oranges. It tends to accumulate in the stratum corneum and in fatty tissues of the dermis. Its color is most obvious in the palms of the hands and soles of the feet, and is most intense when a large amount of carotene-rich food has been consumed.

Hemoglobin is a pigment found in red blood cells that is used to carry oxygen from the lungs to body tissues. The pinkish hue of fair skin is due to the reddish color of oxygenated hemoglobin in blood circulating through dermal capillaries. Because Caucasian skin contains relatively small amounts of melanin, the almost transparent epidermis allows the color of underlying hemoglobin to show through.

Specific circulation patterns of blood flow also can influence skin color. For instance, embarrassment increases blood flow to the skin, particularly in the face and neck regions. This is what leads to *blushing*. An increase in blood flow also can be caused by high blood pressure (*hypertension*), inflammation, or an allergic response. In contrast, a sudden fright or anger can cause a rapid drop in blood flow to the skin, causing its color to blanch. Pale skin also can indicate low blood pressure (*hypotension*), anemia (low red blood cell count), or impaired blood flow.

In addition, hemoglobin changes its color when it releases oxygen. Consequently, poorly oxygenated blood causes skin to take on a bluish hue, a condition known as **cyanosis**. Melanin masks the appearance of cyanosis in dark-skinned people. However, it can still be detected by looking

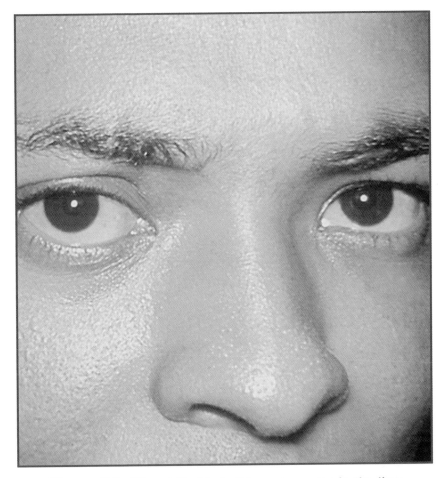

Figure 7.3 When bilirubin builds up in excess in the liver and is distributed to other cells, a condition called jaundice occurs. Jaundice results in a yellowish pigment of the skin and the eyes.

at the color of fingernail beds. Cyanosis is common during heart failure or extreme breathing disorders.

A yellow color (**jaundice**) occurs when bile pigments, such as *bilirubin*, are deposited in body tissues (Figure 7.3). Bilirubin is formed by the liver during the breakdown of worn-out or damaged red blood cells. Thus, jaundice usually indicates a problem with the liver. However, jaundice is common in newborns (called *physiological jaundice*), usually appearing two or three days after birth in over 50% of babies. This occurs because fetal red blood cells are short-lived, and break down rapidly following birth so they can be replaced with adult red blood cells. Frequently, an infant's liver is unable to process the resulting bilirubin fast enough to prevent its accumulation in blood. Usually physiological jaundice in babies is not harmful and disappears by 1 to 2 weeks of age. In most cases, an increase in the supply of breast milk or formula is recommended. However, high levels of bilirubin can cause deafness or brain damage in some babies. These complications can be prevented by lowering bilirubin using phototherapy for a few days (blue light helps break down bilirubin in the skin).

CONNECTIONS

Skin is one of the largest organs of the body, and along with its derivatives (sweat glands, oil glands, hair, and nails) and accessory structures (blood vessels and nerves), forms the integumentary system. The skin forms a barrier that protects the body from dehydration, as well as from physical and chemical insults. In addition, it shields us from continual bacterial invasion and ultraviolet radiation.

Skin has two tissue layers: the epidermis and dermis. The epidermis is composed of stratified squamous epithelium, and is composed of four different cell types: keratinocytes, melanocytes, Langerhan's cells, and Merkel cells. The tough, fibrous protein keratin accumulates in keratinocytes, providing them with their protective qualities. The dermis has two layers: the thinner outer papillary layer of loose (areolar) connective tissue and the deeper, thicker reticular layer, composed of dense connective tissue.

Two main factors contribute to skin color: the quantity and distribution of pigments in the skin, and blood flow. The most important factor in determining melanin production is a person's genetic code. In addition, melanocytes are stimulated by exposure of skin to sunlight, causing them to increase their production of melanin. Specific circulation patterns of blood flow also can influence skin color.

8

Skin Derivatives:
The Integumentary System

The **integumentary system** includes a number of diverse structures derived from the epidermis of skin. These *appendages* include hair, nails, oil glands, and sweat glands. Each has a unique role in helping maintain homeostasis.

HAIR

Hair is an outgrowth of skin that is unique to mammals (Figure 8.1). Its main function is to provide thermal insulation. In this capacity, however, the hairs scattered over the human body are essentially useless. Nonetheless, human hair does provide some important functions. For instance, it protects the scalp from ultraviolet rays and mechanical bumps. Eyelashes shield the eyes, and cause a reflex blinking when unexpectedly touched. Hair lining the respiratory tract and ear canals keep out foreign particles. In addition, hair has a significant sensory role because receptors associated with *follicles* are sensitive to touch.

For humans, hair is present on all skin surfaces, except the palms of the hands, soles of the feet, lips, nipples, and parts of the external genitalia. Humans have three different types of hair: **lanugo**, **vellus**, and **terminal**. *Lanugo* is the soft, fine hair that covers a fetus beginning around the third or fourth month after conception. It falls off about a month before birth, and is replaced by a second coat that is shed a few months after birth. *Vellus hair* also is soft and fine. However, unlike lanugo, it grows and persists

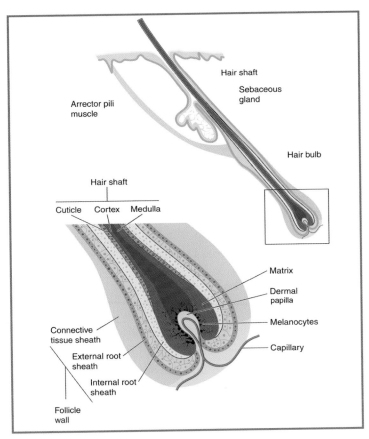

Figure 8.1 Structure of a hair and hair follicle. The region of a hair that projects from the skin is the shaft, whereas the embedded portion is called the root. The hair follicle extends from the epidermis into the dermis, and its deep end is expanded, forming a hair bulb (enlarged in the diagram). Hair is produced in the bulb by active cell division in a single layer of epidermal cells called the matrix, which is nourished by a knot of capillaries in the dermal papilla. The hair shaft has a central core, the medulla (consists of large cells and air spaces), which is surrounded by the cortex (several layers of flattened cells). The outermost cuticle is formed from a single layer of cells.

throughout life, covering most of the body surface. *Terminal hair* is thick and strong. It forms eyebrows and eyelashes, and is found on the scalp. During adolescence, in response to changing hormone levels, many vellus hairs of the armpits and pubic area are replaced with terminal hairs. In males, the same is true for the face, chest, legs, forearms, back, and shoulders.

Each terminal hair consists of a central core called the *medulla* (fine hair lacks a medulla). The medulla is surrounded by the *cortex*, which in turn is enclosed by a *cuticle*. The cuticle is formed by a single layer of cells that overlap one another like shingles on a roof. This arrangement helps keep hairs from matting or tangling with each other. The cuticle can wear away with continual exposure to the elements and abrasion, allowing the underlying cortex to frizz, forming "split ends." The cuticle also can be damaged by exposure to chlorinated water in swimming pools.

Hair has both a *shaft* and a *root*. The shaft projects above the surface of the skin. In contrast, the root extends below the surface into the dermis, where it is embedded in a group of cells called a **hair follicle**. The follicle is really a compound structure, meaning it is composed of several parts. Its inner layer is a flexible sheath composed of epithelial cells that are

DID YOU KNOW?

Hair color, like skin color, is genetically determined by the amount and type of pigment produced, which accumulates in the cortex. For instance, hair is dark in color in the presence of abundant melanin. In contrast, lighter color hair results when little melanin is synthesized. Interestingly, true red hair depends on a separate reddish pigment, which also can influence the overall affect of melanin. For instance, auburn hair is produced by a combination of red pigment mixed with relatively large amounts of melanin. In contrast, strawberry blonde hair results when red pigment mixes with little melanin. Gray hair, associated with age, is actually caused by a decrease in the production of melanin, and a corresponding increase in the number and size of air pockets in the hair shaft. Light striking the air pockets gives hair a gray sheen.

responsible for producing hair. The outer layer is composed of dermal connective tissue. It provides blood vessels and physical reinforcement. The inferior end (bottom) of a hair follicle is enlarged, forming a structure called the **hair bulb**. Each hair bulb is wrapped by a knot of sensory nerve endings, the **hair root plexus**. This anatomical arrangement allows hair to act as a sensitive touch receptor permitting us, for instance, to feel insects crawling on our skin (hopefully before they have a chance to sting or bite us).

Hair is formed by division of cells in the **matrix**, a growth zone located in the hair bulb. The matrix displays active mitosis because it is continuous with the stratum basale, the epidermal layer capable of cell division. The newly formed cells are nourished by blood vessels located in the **papilla**, which is an indentation of the dermal connective tissue at the base of the follicle. As daughter cells continue to divide, they are pushed farther away from the growing region and also become keratinized. Shortly thereafter they die. Thus, the bulk of hair is composed of non-living cells.

Hair growth depends on several factors, including nutritional status, gender, and age, as well as circulating levels of some hormones. For instance, poor nutrition will result in poor hair growth. In addition, the hormone testosterone encourages growth of hair. Although scalp hair typically grows an average of 2 millimeters per week, each follicle goes through a series of growth cycles. Initially, there is an *active phase*, which generally lasts 2 to 6 years. This is followed by a *resting phase*, where the follicle is inactive for several months. Following the resting phase, the matrix proliferates again, forming a new hair that will replace the old one, which has already fallen out or will be pushed out. Because follicles generally spend more time in an active phase, we only shed about 90 hairs from our scalp each day. Interestingly, the active phase for eyebrow hair is only three to four months long. This explains why eyebrow hair is much shorter than scalp hair.

Hair growth is generally fastest from the teen years to the forties. However, after that it slows down, and hairs are not replaced as fast as they are shed. This leads to hair thinning, which occurs in both sexes. However, true baldness, usually known as **male pattern baldness**, is a genetically determined condition influenced by the presence of male hormones. That is, true baldness is caused by a delayed action gene, which is turned on in adulthood, thereby changing the response of hair follicles to circulating levels of testosterone. As a result, hair follicles shrink, and the length of time spent in a growth cycle decreases. In fact, growth cycles can become so short, hair does not have a chance to emerge before it is shed. In addition, thick terminal hairs are replaced by soft, fine vellus hairs. This change occurs in a characteristic pattern, beginning at the forehead and temple, and eventually reaching the crown. Interestingly, a drug originally used to treat high blood pressure (minoxidil) was accidentally found to stimulate hair growth in some individuals. The lotion appears to work by

DID YOU KNOW?

The **arrector pili** is a tiny smooth muscle in the dermis attached to a hair follicle. If a person is emotionally upset or cold, nerve impulses may stimulate this muscle to contract, causing it to pull on a follicle, thereby decreasing its angle with the skin surface. This, in turn, generates goose bumps. Although this action does not play a significant role in humans, it does keep other mammals warm in cold weather by increasing the thickness of their insulation. Contraction of arrector pili muscles also is used for body language signals. For instance, a scared cat looks larger when its fur stands on end, and a dog sends a clear message that it should not be touched when it raises the hair on the back of its neck while baring its teeth.

increasing blood flow to the scalp, thereby stimulating the activity of existing follicles.

CUTANEOUS GLANDS

The **cutaneous** glands are all *exocrine* glands that secrete to the skin surface via ducts. There are two main types: *sebaceous glands* and *sweat glands*. Both reside almost entirely in the dermis, but are formed by cells of the stratum basale (an epidermal layer).

Oil glands

Oil glands or **sebaceous glands** are found all over the body, except the palms of the hands and soles of the feet. Although they are an epidermal derivative, the secretory part of the gland is located in the dermis. In some cases, the glands open directly onto the skin surface. However, in most instances they open into hair follicles.

Sebaceous glands secrete an oily substance called **sebum**, which is made of fats, cholesterol, protein, and salts. Sebum is used to lubricate hair and skin. It also protects skin against desiccation. In addition, sebum contains anti-bacterial chemicals, which help prevent bacteria normally present on the skin surface from invading deeper regions. Unfortunately, the ducts of oil glands can become blocked, allowing sebum and bacteria to accumulate. This results in acne (refer to Chapter 9 for a further discussion of this topic).

Sweat glands

Sweat glands or **sudoriferous glands** are widely distributed in the skin. In fact, each person has about 2.5 million. There are two main types: *eccrine* and *apocrine*. **Eccrine glands** produce their secretions in coiled structures located in the dermis, and then dump their contents (*sweat*) directly on the skin surface via a pore. They are most numerous in the skin of the forehead, palms, and soles. In contrast, they are absent in the lips, eardrums, nail beds, and portions of the external genitalia.

Sweat is mostly composed of water. It also contains some salts, lactic acid, vitamin C, and metabolic wastes, such as urea and ammonia. The principal function of sweat is to help regulate body temperature through the evaporation of water on the skin surface. In fact, on a hot day one can easily lose several liters of body water in this way. In addition, the slightly acidic pH of sweat inhibits growth of bacteria.

Apocrine glands are a type of sweat gland, mainly located in the armpits and pubic region. They are usually larger than eccrine glands, and empty their contents into hair follicles. Although their secretion contains all the substances present in eccrine sweat, they also contain additional fatty acids and proteins. These substances make the secretion more *viscous* (thick), and also gives it a whitish-yellowish color. Apocrine secretion is typically odorless. However, bacterial action on the skin surface converts its proteins and fats into compounds that release an unpleasant odor. In fact, antiperspirants are designed to inhibit such secretions, whereas deodorants mask their odor.

Apocrine glands do not function until puberty, at which time they are stimulated by a rise in sex hormones (testosterone and estrogen). Although their exact function is not known, they generally become most active when a person is emotionally upset or excited, such as when frightened, in pain, or sexually aroused. Apocrine glands also enlarge and shrink with the phases of a woman's menstrual cycle. It is therefore unlikely these glands play a significant role in temperature regulation. Instead, it is generally assumed that apocrine glands are analogous to the sexual scent glands of other animals, and they also may play a scent role during a *fight or flight response*. It has been suggested that pubic and axillary (under arm) hair help disperse the odor of apocrine secretions; that is, a way of enhancing the spread of one's scent.

Ceruminous glands are modified apocrine glands found in the lining of the external ear canal. They secrete a thick, sticky substance called **cerumen** or earwax. Along with tiny hairs in the ear canal, this substance deters insects and blocks the entry of foreign substances.

Modified sweat glands specialized to secrete milk are called **mammary glands.** Although they are present in both genders, mammary glands normally only function in females. In non-pregnant women, the glandular structure is largely undeveloped and the duct system is rudimentary. However, under stimulation of the hormone *prolactin,* which is secreted from the pituitary gland during pregnancy, the glandular tissue develops the ability to form milk.

NAILS

Nails are protective coverings on the ends of the fingers and toes. Like hair, nails are modified skin tissue (stratified squamous epithelium), which has been hardened by the protein keratin. However, nails differ from hair in that they grow continuously. Also, compared to hair, nail growth is relatively slow. Whereas hair can grow 5 to 6 inches per year, fingernails grow about 1.5 inches per year, and toenails about 0.5 inches.

Nail cells form in a region called the *nail root,* which is embedded in skin (Figure 8.2). The growing region is the **lunula,** the whitish, crescent-moon-shaped area at the base of a nail. As a nail develops, it slides forward over a layer of epithelium, the **nail bed,** which is continuous with the stratum basale. The free edge of a nail extends over the tip of a finger or toe and is the part we trim. The border of a nail is overlapped with skin folds, and the *proximal* nail fold is called the **cuticle.** Most of a nail appears pink due to the influence of blood vessels in the dermis below. The lunula, however, looks white because it has a thickened matrix, which obscures underlying tissue.

ORGAN SYSTEM INTEGRATION

No system in the body acts independently of the others. In fact, all systems must be integrated in order to maintain

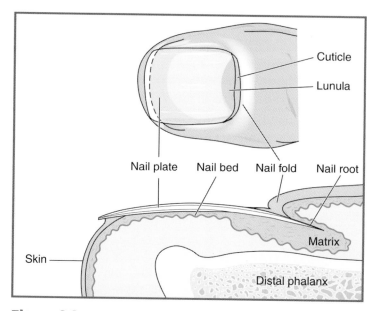

Figure 8.2 Nails are composed of hardened stratified squamous epithelial cells. The different parts of the nail are shown in the diagram here. Nails form in the nail root and grow along the nail bed. The cuticle is comprised of the proximal nail fold, and the white, crescent-shaped area is called the lunula.

homeostasis, and the integumentary system is no exception. Recall that skin is able to synthesize vitamin D when exposed to sunlight. However, this form of vitamin D does not have significant biological activity. Rather, it must be metabolized into an active hormone, first by a chemical modification (hydroxylation reaction) in the liver, followed by a second hydroxylation in the kidneys. Vitamin D promotes absorption of dietary calcium by the small intestine. In turn, calcium is necessary for the proper formation of bones and teeth, as well as for blood clotting and the normal function of nerve and muscle tissues. Thus, by providing the body with vitamin D, the integumentary system is linked to the activity of the digestive, skeletal, muscular, nervous, cardiovascular, and renal systems.

The integumentary system also contains receptors sensitive to touch, pressure, temperature, and pain. These receptors provide the nervous system with important information about our external environment. The nervous system in return controls the activity of sweat glands and blood flow, thereby using the skin as a means to help regulate body temperature. Further, the activity of sebaceous and apocrine glands is influenced by sex hormones released from the endocrine system. Thus, the integumentary system also is integrated with the endocrine and reproductive systems.

CONNECTIONS

The integumentary system includes a number of diverse structures derived from the epidermis of skin, including hair, nails, oil glands, and sweat glands. Hair is an outgrowth of skin unique to mammals. It protects the scalp from ultraviolet rays and mechanical bumps, keeps foreign particles out of the respiratory tract, and has a sensory role. Each terminal hair consists of a central core called the medulla, which is surrounded by the cortex and enclosed by a cuticle. Hair is embedded in a group of cells called a follicle, which has an inner layer of epithelial cells responsible for producing hair and an outer layer of dermal connective tissue that provides blood vessels and physical reinforcement.

Sebaceous glands secrete sebum, an oily substance that lubricates hair and inhibits the growth of bacteria. Eccrine glands produce sweat, which helps regulate body temperature through the evaporation of water on the skin surface. Apocrine glands are a type of sweat gland, mainly located in the armpits and pubic region. They do not function until puberty, and are assumed to be analogous to the sexual scent glands of other animals. Ceruminous glands are modified apocrine glands found in the lining of the external ear canal that produce earwax, whereas mammary glands are modified sweat glands specialized to secrete milk.

9

Common Skin Disorders:

When Homeostasis is Challenged

There are over 1,000 different ailments of the skin! The most common skin disorders result from allergies and from bacterial, viral, and fungal infections. Less common, but more serious skin problems include burns and cancers.

ALLERGIES

An **allergy** (also called *hypersensitivity*) occurs when a normally harmless substance, called an *allergen*, evokes an inappropriate immune response. In fact, it is this reaction that causes tissue damage, as the body responds to a harmless item. An **immediate hypersensitivity** describes a response (*anaphylaxis*) that occurs within seconds or minutes after contacting an allergen, such as allergic response to bee venom, dust, pollen, or certain food items.

The primary immune culprits for many immediate hyper-sensitivities are **mast cells** and **basophils**, white blood cells that release **histamine** and other inflammatory chemicals. Although these chemicals play a beneficial role during an acute inflammation or infection, they are inappropriately released during an immediate hypersensitivity. Histamine causes small blood vessels in the area of exposure to dilate (widen) and become leaky. As a result, the affected region becomes red and swollen in response to increased blood flow and to fluid accumulation in the extracellular matrix. In addition, histamine may make the affected area feel itchy. Thus, histamine is largely responsible for the typical symptoms of anaphylaxis: a runny nose, hives, and watery eyes. Treatment usually includes administration of an antihistamine agent which blocks histamine release.

A **delayed hypersensitivity** reaction refers to an allergy that usually takes several days to appear. A familiar example is *contact dermatitis*. This refers to itching, redness, and swelling of skin caused by exposure to substances, such as poison ivy or a certain cosmetic chemical, which provoke an allergic response in sensitive individuals (Figure 9.1). In this case, white blood cells known as *lymphocytes* inappropriately respond by releasing chemicals called *lymphokines*. Thus, antihistamines would not be helpful in treating a delayed hypersensitivity. Instead, corticosteroid drugs are used. They provide relief by inhibiting the release of lymphokines.

YOUR HEALTH: Anaphylactic Shock

Often an immediate hypersensitivity is simply an annoyance, as with hay fever (an allergic response to pollen). However, in some instances, an allergy may be life threatening when an allergen directly enters the blood stream, such as with a bee sting or drug injection. Unfortunately, this situation may lead to a systemic (body wide) response in susceptible individuals called *anaphylactic shock*. In this case, mast cells and basophils throughout the body are inappropriately activated. As a result, there is a sudden dilation of blood vessels, accompanied with fluid loss from the bloodstream, which leads to circulatory collapse. In addition, airways constrict, making it difficult to breathe. This condition may be fatal if untreated. Individuals suffering from anaphylactic shock are usually given an injection of adrenaline, a hormone that quickly reverses the histamine-mediated events. This is then followed by an oral antihistamine.

Figure 9.1 Poison ivy leaves, pictured here, contain oils which can cause an allergic reaction in humans. When the body is exposed to these oils, white blood cells called lymphocytes release chemicals that cause itching, redness, and swelling. This response is known as contact dermatitis.

INFECTIONS

Skin infections can be caused by bacteria, viruses, and fungi. A fairly common bacterial infection is **impetigo**, which is characterized by pink, water-filled raised lesions that develop a yellow crust and eventually rupture. Impetigo is highly contagious and relatively common in young school-aged children. A bacterial infection of a hair follicle and/or sebaceous glands can cause a **boil** to form. This can spread to the underlying hypodermis and cause a fair amount of discomfort. Two common fungal infections of skin include **athlete's foot** and *ringworm* (Figure 9.2). Both are characterized by an itchy, red, peeling condition, and are treated with anti-fungal agents.

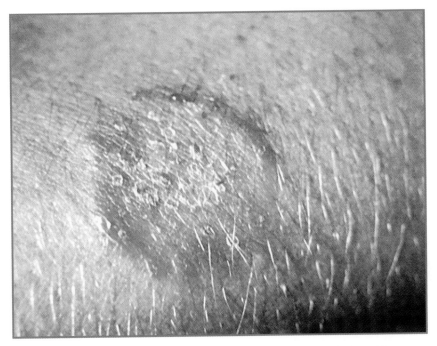

Figure 9.2 **Ringworm is a common infection of the skin. Contrary to its name, the disease is caused by a fungus, not a worm. The fungus can cause a circular, red, itchy rash, as can be seen in the picture here. Ringworm can be treated with anti-fungal medications.**

Cold sores (fever blisters) are small, fluid-filled blisters that itch and sting. They are caused by a *herpes simplex* viral infection. The virus localizes in a cutaneous nerve, where it remains dormant until activated by emotional upset, fever, or ultraviolet radiation. Cold sores usually occur around the lips and in the soft, moist lining of the mouth. A related herpes simplex virus causes genital herpes, a sexually transmitted disease, which can be spread to the mouth. (Note that measles and mononucleosis are both causes by different types of herpes simplex viruses). As stated previously, human papilloma viruses stimulate rapid cell division in the stratum basale, which leads to the formation of a wart (a benign tumor).

ACNE

About four out of five teenagers are afflicted with **acne**, a skin condition that affects hair follicles and sebaceous glands (Figure 9.3). For this reason, acne occurs on areas of the body where oil glands are largest and most numerous: the face, chest, upper back, and shoulders. Adolescents are most prone to developing acne because oil glands increase their size and production of sebum in response to increasing levels of *androgens* (male hormones) that occur during puberty. Androgens are secreted by endocrine cells in the testes, ovaries, and adrenal glands. Because males generally have higher levels of circulating androgens than females, their acne is typically more severe. However, acne can flare up in women around the time of menstruation, when levels of the hormone progesterone have increased following ovulation.

Acne is essentially an inflammation that results when sebum and dead cells clog an oil gland duct entering a hair follicle. A follicle obstructed in this manner forms a *whitehead*. Sometimes the sebum in plugged follicles oxidizes and mixes with melanin, causing a *blackhead* to form. The next stage of acne is typically a red, raised bump, often with a white dot of pus in the center. It appears when obstructed follicles rupture and spew their contents into the surrounding epidermis. This small infection (a pimple) usually heals in a week or two. However, in severe cases of acne, the rupture of plugged follicles can produce large cysts that extend into the dermis, which may leave a scar when healed.

Contrary to popular belief, acne is not caused by eating certain foods, such as chocolate, pizza, and potato chips (although there are other health concerns with a typical teenage diet that is generally high in saturated fat and low in fruits and vegetables). In addition, because follicles plug from below, dirt or oil on the skin surface is not responsible for causing acne. Nonetheless, washing your face with warm water will help open plugged follicles. It also turns out that acne has

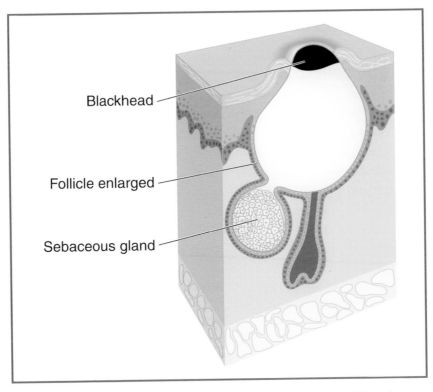

Figure 9.3 Acne is a common teenage skin affliction. Although many myths surround the condition, acne is not caused by eating excessive amounts of junk food. During adolescence, the body increases its production of sebum. This excess sebum can mix with dead cells and become trapped in a hair follicle. When the sebum oxidizes and mixes with melanin, a blackhead will form, as is shown in this diagram.

a genetic link. In other words, individuals are more likely to develop acne if their parents had this problem. Also, acne is more likely to flare up during times of stress, presumably due to stress-induced changes in hormone levels.

Treatment for acne includes some topical agents, which are applied directly to the skin. For example, benzoyl peroxide is commonly used because it is a powerful antibacterial agent that kills bacteria living in hair follicles. Severe cases of acne may require oral medication, such as an antibiotic agent that inhibits bacteria inhabiting follicles.

SKIN CANCER

Skin cancer is the most common type of cancer. An important risk factor in developing this disease is overexposure to ultraviolet rays in sunlight. This ionizing form of radiation can locally suppress the immune system, making it more difficult for the body to fight formation of cancer cells. Ultraviolet radiation also has sufficient energy to alter the structure of DNA thereby causing mutations. In addition, some cases of chronic irritation of the skin by infections, chemicals, or physical trauma may be a risk factor for skin cancer.

Cancer arising in epithelial tissue is called a **carcinoma**, and it accounts for over 90% of all cancers. Cutaneous (skin) carcinomas are the most common type of skin cancers. They occur most frequently in light-skinned people over the age of forty, especially in those who have been exposed to sunlight on a regular basis, such as farmers, construction workers, and sunbathers. In addition, episodes of severe sunburn during childhood appear to predispose individuals to developing skin cancer many years later. That is why it is important to practice cancer prevention at an early age.

The least malignant and most common form of skin

YOUR HEALTH: Skin Cancer

The American Cancer Society suggests the **ABCD rule** when checking for skin cancer. A: *asymmetry*, because most melanomas are irregular in shape. B: *border*, because melanomas often have diffuse, unclear borders. C: *color*, because melanomas usually have a mottled appearance, containing brown, black, red, white, or blue colors. D: *diameter*, because growths with a diameter of more than 5 millimeters (about 0.2 inches) are life threatening.

cancer is **basal cell carcinoma**. In fact, over 30% of Caucasians develop this type of cancer in their lifetime. Basal cell carcinoma originates in the actively dividing cells of the stratum basale, usually in sun-exposed areas of the face. Although it can invade the dermis and hypodermis, it is a slow growing cancer. Surgical removal is prescribed, and usually provides a full cure if caught before the cancer has spread. **Squamous cell carcinoma** arises from the keratinocytes of the stratum spinosum, usually on the scalp, ears, lower lip, and hands. It tends to grow rapidly, and will metastasize if not removed. However, if caught early and surgically removed, the chance of a complete cure is good.

Cancer of melanocytes is called **melanoma**. This is the most dangerous form of skin cancer. Melanomas can appear spontaneously or develop from a pre-existing mole. They form most often in light-skinned people who tend to burn rather than tan. In addition, short, intermittent exposure to high-intensity sunlight appears to initiate these growths. For instance, melanomas are not uncommon in people who stay indoors most of the time, but occasionally sustain blistering sunburns. This form of cancer metastasizes quickly into lymph and blood vessels. Therefore, the key to survival is early detection. The usual treatment is surgical removal and chemotherapy.

To reduce the chances of developing skin cancer, avoid excessive exposure to ultraviolet light, especially during the midday hours when the sun's rays are at their strongest. Wearing a wide-brimmed hat will help keep sunlight off your face and neck. In addition, use sunscreens that have a sun protection factor (SPF) of at least 15. Keep in mind that ultraviolet rays can pass through clouds, penetrate water up to about three feet, and reflect off surfaces, such as sand and a patio deck. Further, tanning salons also expose individuals to ultraviolet light, especially to a form of ultraviolet light called UV-A, which has been shown to suppress the immune system. Finally, examine skin regularly for abnormal growths, particularly those that change color, shape, or surface texture.

BURNS

A *burn* refers to tissue damage caused by intense heat, electricity, radiation, or certain chemicals, all of which **denature** proteins, thereby leading to cell death. Burns are classified according to the depth to which the tissue damage penetrates (Figure 9.4). *First-degree burns* are confined to the upper layers of epidermis. The affected area becomes red and swollen. These burns are generally not serious, and heal in a few days. A mild sunburn is an example of a first-degree burn.

Damage from a *second-degree burn* extends through the epidermis into the upper region of the dermis. As a result, blisters appear. Because sufficient epithelium remains intact, regeneration of skin can occur, and no permanent scars will result if care is taken to prevent infection. *Third-degree burns*, on the other hand, extend all the way through the epidermis, and dermis, into underlying subcutaneous tissues. The burned area appears blanched or blackened. Strangely enough, third-degree burns do not hurt initially because nerve endings in the dermis are destroyed. Unfortunately, regeneration of skin is not possible. Therefore, skin grafting is necessary to cover the underlying exposed tissues.

Severe burns, particularly those covering large portions of the body, are life threatening. The immediate problem concerns loss of fluids containing proteins and electrolytes, resulting from the loss of an effective waterproof barrier. Sufficient dehydration and electrolyte imbalance will lead to shutdown of the kidneys and also to circulatory shock from inadequate circulation of blood (caused by a low fluid volume). In this case, fluids must be replaced immediately. In addition, many calories are needed to replace those lost as proteins. Consequently, severe burn patients are given supplementary nutrients through gastric tubes and intravenous lines.

Once fluid volumes have been restored, infection becomes the most important threat. In fact, infection is the leading cause of death in burn victims. Burned skin is sterile

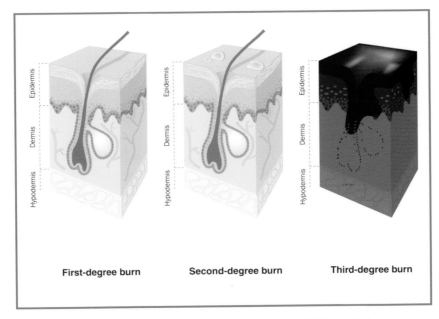

First-degree burn   Second-degree burn   Third-degree burn

Figure 9.4 A burn is caused when heat, electricity, radiation, or caustic chemicals denature proteins and cause cell death. First-degree burns occur when only the top layer of skin, the epidermis, is affected. Burns which penetrate the dermis are considered second-degree burns. The burn can heal completely, but some scarring may occur. Third-degree burns occur when cells the subcutaneous tissue (hypodermis) is affected. Hair follicles and nerve endings may be damaged, and skin regeneration is not usually likely.

for about 24 hours. However, soon thereafter, opportunistic bacteria and fungi easily invade areas where skin has been destroyed. The situation is exacerbated by depression of the immune system, which usually occurs within one or two days after a severe burn.

BIRTHMARKS

It is not uncommon for people to be born with red birthmarks, called **port wine stains**. Their cause is not known, however, they contain an abnormally dense collection of dermal blood vessels, usually on the face or neck. As the body grows, so does the birthmark. In some cases, the mark darkens with age, and it also may develop a bumpy texture due to nodules of blood vessels. Although there is no known health risk associated with birthmarks, there may be a psychological aspect. Laser therapy is often used to remove these blemishes.

ROSACEA

Rosacea is characterized by engorgement of blood vessels, especially of the cheeks and nose. The disorder causes persistent flushing of facial skin, which appears red and inflamed, and also is marked with whitehead-like bumps and spidery blood vessels. It tends to strike most often between the ages of 30 and 50. Although it is more common in women, its symptoms are more acute in men. The disorder is exacerbated with consumption of alcohol and spicy foods, and also by exposure to sunlight. It appears that rosacea results from skin infection with *Helicobacter pylori*, a bacterium that also causes stomach ulcers. Untreated, rosacea gradually and painlessly disfigures the skin with patches of swollen veins and clusters of pustules. Those afflicted are often given antibiotics. They also may seek laser treatment to destroy swollen blood vessels.

BED SORES

Long-term restriction of blood flow to the skin will result in death of cells. If severe enough, skin ulcers (*bedsores*) will form. This problem is most common in bedridden individuals who are not turned regularly, or who are repeatedly dragged across a bed. The weight of body parts puts pressure on skin, especially over bony projections. Because this restricts blood supply, the skin becomes blanched (pale) at these locations. If the situation is not corrected, cells will eventually die, leading to breaks in the skin at compressed sites. Permanent damage to the superficial blood flow eventually results in degeneration and ulceration of skin.

CONNECTIONS

The most common skin disorders result from bacterial (impetigo, acne, boils), viral (cold sore, wart), and fungal (ringworm) infections, and from allergies. An allergy occurs when a normally harmless substance, an allergen, evokes an inappropriate immune response. An immediate hypersensitivity refers to a response within minutes after contacting an allergen, and is caused by inappropriate release of histamine from mast cells. Contact dermatitis, such as poison ivy, results from release of lymphokines from lymphocytes.

Skin cancer is the most common type of cancer. An important risk factor in developing this disease is overexposure to ultraviolet rays in sunlight. Cancer arising in epithelial tissue is called a carcinoma, and it accounts for over 90% of all cancers. The least malignant and most common form of skin cancer is basal cell carcinoma. Squamous cell carcinoma arises from the keratinocytes of the stratum spinosum, usually on the scalp, ears, lower lip, and hands. Cancer of melanocytes is called melanoma. This is the most dangerous form of skin cancer.

A burn refers to tissue damage caused by intense heat, electricity, radiation, or certain chemicals, all of which denature proteins, thereby leading to cell death. First-degree burns are confined to the upper layers of epidermis, whereas second-degree burns extend through the epidermis into the upper region of the dermis. Third-degree burns extend all the way through the epidermis and dermis, into underlying subcutaneous tissues. Severe burns can be life threatening because of resulting fluid loss and infection.

Glossary

ABCD rule List of suggestions provided by The American Cancer Society when checking for skin cancer.

Acne Inflammation that results when sebum and dead cells clog an oil gland duct entering a hair follicle.

Active transport Membrane transport processes that require ATP, usually refers to solute pumping against a concentration gradient.

Adipose tissue Loose connective tissue modified to store fat.

Albinism An inherited disorder characterized by the inability of melanocytes to produce melanin.

Allergy Inappropriate and overzealous immune response to a substance (allergen) that otherwise would be harmless.

Anaphase Third stage of mitosis where a full set of daughter chromosomes moves to opposite spindle poles.

Anucleate Without a nucleus.

Apical surface Outer surface of epithelial tissue that is exposed to the external environment or a body cavity.

Apocrine gland Type of sweat gland that produces a secretion of water, salts, proteins, and fatty acids in response to anger or sexual excitement.

Apoptosis Programmed cell death, characterized by destruction of chromatin and the nuclear envelope.

Areolar tissue Loose connective tissue found throughout the body, acts as packing material and glue.

Arrector pili Tiny, smooth muscles attached to hair follicles that contract in response to cold or fear, causing goosebumps.

Athlete's foot A fungal infection of the feet characterized by itchy, red, peeling skin.

ATP (adenosine triphosphate) Organic molecule that stores and releases energy for use by cells.

Basal cell carcinoma Most common form of skin cancer that originates in the actively dividing cells of the stratum basale, usually in sun-exposed areas of the face.

Basal lamina Non-living supporting layer of the basement membrane secreted by epithelial cells.

Basal surface Inner surface of epithelial tissue that is anchored to the basement membrane.

Basement membrane Extracellular material consisting of the basal lamina secreted by epithelial cells and the reticular lamina secreted by connective tissue cells.

Basophil A type of white blood cell that releases histamine.

Benign Term referring to tumors that lack the ability to invade surrounding tissues; not malignant.

Biconcave Having two depressions, one on either side of a disk-shaped cell.

Bilayer Two layers, usually referring to the phospholipid layers of a cell membrane.

Boil A bacterial infection of a hair follicle and/or sebaceous gland.

Carbohydrate Organic compound composed of carbon, hydrogen, and oxygen; includes sugars, glycogen, and starch.

Cancer A malignant mass of altered cells that divide abnormally and are capable of spreading to other body parts.

Carcinogen A chemical or agent that causes cancer.

Carcinoma Tumor that arises in epithelial tissue.

Cardiac muscle A contractile tissue only found in the heart wall.

Carotene A yellow-orange pigment found in many food items capable of accumulating in the stratum corneum of skin.

Carrier Term used to describe a membrane protein that moves substances by facilitated diffusion.

Cartilage A connective tissue composed of chondrocytes and a solid, flexible matrix.

Cell The smallest unit having the properties of life.

Cell adhesion molecule Membrane protein that links cells together.

Cell-cell recognition Ability of the receptors of one cell type to recognize glycoproteins of another cell.

Cell cycle Events a cell undergoes from the time it forms until it completes a division.

Glossary

Cell theory The concept that all organisms consist of one or more cells, the cell is the smallest unit with the capacity of independent life, and all cells arise from pre-existing cells.

Centriole Small structure that gives rise to microtubules of cilia, flagella, and spindle fibers.

Cerumin A sticky, bitter substance, also called earwax.

Ceruminous gland Modified apocrine gland found in the lining of the external ear, produces earwax.

Channel Term use to describe a membrane protein that forms an aqueous pore in a membrane through which ions can traverse.

Cholesterol A type of lipid found in most animal fats and cell membranes. It is synthesized by the liver.

Chondrocyte Mature connective tissue cell type that forms cartilage.

Chromatin A molecule of DNA and all the proteins associated with it.

Chromosome Bar-like bodies of tightly coiled chromatin that are visible during cell division.

Cilium Tiny, motile, hair-like projection on a cell surface.

Cleavage furrow Indentation of a cell membrane during cytokinesis, caused by contraction of a ring of microfilaments over the midline of the spindle.

Cold sore Small, fluid-filled blisters caused by a herpes simplex viral infection that itch and sting.

Collagen The most abundant protein fiber found in the extracellular matrix of connective tissue.

Columnar Cylindrical or shaped like a column.

Concentration gradient Difference in concentration (number of solute particles per unit volume of solvent) of a particular substance between two different areas.

Connective tissue A primary tissue form that includes bone, cartilage, adipose, and blood.

Contact dermatitis Itching, redness, and swelling of skin caused by exposure to substances that provokes an allergic response in sensitive individuals.

Cuboidal Cube-like shape.

Cutaneous Pertaining to the skin.

Cutaneous membrane A term used to describe skin; however, the term is misleading because skin is actually an organ.

Cuticle Fold of skin projecting over the proximal end of nails.

Cyanosis A bluish skin color resulting from poorly oxygenated hemoglobin.

Cytokinesis Division of the cytoplasm, usually follows nuclear division.

Cytoplasm The cellular material surrounding the nucleus and enclosed by the plasma membrane.

Cytoskeleton A dynamic and elaborate series of internal rods in the cytosol, which support cellular structures, help maintains cell shape, and provide the machinery to generate various cell movements.

Cytosol The viscous, semitransparent fluid substance of the cytoplasm in which other structures are suspended.

Delayed hypersensitivity Allergic reaction that usually occurs in sensitized individuals after 24 to 48 hours of exposure to an allergen, mainly caused by lymphokine release from lymphocytes.

Denature The unfolding of proteins, causing them to lose their specific three-dimensional shape; this results from the breaking of hydrogen bonds when a protein is exposed to high temperature or low pH.

Dermis Layer of skin beneath the epidermis; composed of dense connective tissue.

Differentiation Ability of cells to develop particular characteristics by expressing specific genes and repressing others.

Diffusion The spreading of particles from an area of higher concentration to a region of lower concentration, using kinetic energy to generate movement.

DNA (deoxyribonucleic acid) A macromolecule in the shape of a double helix, found in the nucleus of cells and carries hereditary information.

Eccrine gland Abundant sweat glands whose secretion is primarily used for temperature regulation.

Glossary

Elastic cartilage Cartilage containing an abundance of elastic fibers, which gives the tissue a great tolerance to repeated bending.

Elastic fiber Long, thin protein fibers found in the extracellular matrix of connective tissue.

Elastin A resilient, rubber-like protein secreted into the extracellular space by connective tissue cells.

Electromagnetic radiation A form of energy that travels in waves and is capable of moving through a vacuum; includes x-rays, ultraviolet rays, visible light, infrared radiation, and radio waves.

Electron microscope A device that uses a beam of electrons to magnify the image of a specimen.

Element A fundamental form of matter that cannot be normally broken down into another substance having different properties.

Endocrine gland Ductless glands that secrete hormones into the blood stream.

Endocytosis Method of vesicular transport by which fairly large extracellular substances enter cells.

Endoplasmic reticulum Organelle that is a membranous network of tubular and sac-like channels in the cytoplasm that modifies newly formed proteins and synthesizes lipids.

Enzyme A biologically generated organic molecule that increases the rate of a chemical reaction.

Epidermis Outer layer of skin composed of keratinized, stratified squamous epithelium.

Epithelial tissue (epithelium) A primary group of cells that covers the body surface and lines its internal cavities, tubes, and organs, and forms glands.

Equilibrium Point at which there is no net change in a chemical reaction or movement by diffusion.

Erythrocyte A red blood cell.

Exocrine gland Gland that secretes into a duct or tube to a free epithelial surface.

Exocytosis Method of vesicular transport by which fairly large intracellular substances exit cells.

Extracellular matrix Nonliving material secreted by connective tissue cells, containing protein fibers and ground substance; used to separate living cells.

Facilitated diffusion Passive transport mechanism that uses a protein carrier.

Fatty acid Linear chain of carbon and hydrogen atoms with an organic acid group at one end.

Fibroblast Actively dividing cell that forms loose and dense connective tissues.

Fibrocartilage Cartilage found in vertebral discs and the knee joint.

First-degree burn Burn confined to the upper layers of epidermis, such as a mild sunburn.

Flagellum Long, whip-like extension on a cell surface that propels sperm.

Fluid mosaic model Idea that cell membranes consist of a phospholipid bilayer in which proteins are dispersed.

Free radical Highly reactive chemicals containing unpaired electrons that can alter the structure of proteins, lipids, and nucleic acids.

Gamete Germ cell (sperm or ovum) that contains half the normal number of chromosomes.

Gene A unit of hereditary information found in chromatin.

Glycocalyx A layer of extracellular-facing glycoproteins on a plasma membrane that act as biological markers.

Glycolipid A lipid molecule with one or more sugars covalently bonded to it.

Glycoprotein A protein molecule with one or more sugars covalently bonded to it.

Golgi apparatus Membranous organelle that sorts and packages proteins for export.

Ground substance Nonliving intercellular material of the extracellular matrix that is secreted by connective tissue cells.

Hair bulb The deep end of a follicle that is expanded.

Hair follicle A compound structure of epidermis and dermis that surrounds a hair root and forms new hair.

Glossary

Hair root plexus A knot of sensory nerve endings that wraps around each hair bulb.

Hemoglobin Iron-containing pigment in red blood cells used to transport oxygen.

Histology The study of tissues and their microscopic structure.

Histamine A chemical released by mast cells that causes vasodilation and increased vascular permeability.

Homeostasis The relatively stable internal environment of the body resulting from the activity of organ systems.

Hyaline cartilage The most abundant type of cartilage that provides firm support with some flexibility.

Hydrophilic A polar substances that dissolves in water.

Hydrophobic A nonpolar substance that is water insoluble.

Hydrostatic pressure Pressure exerted by the volume of a fluid against a wall that encloses the fluid, such as the pressure generated in blood vessels when the heart contracts.

Hypertonic solution A fluid that has a higher osmotic pressure than body fluids and therefore causes cells to lose water and shrink.

Hypotonic solution A fluid that has a lower osmotic pressure than body fluids and therefore causes cells to gain water and swell.

Impetigo A fairly common, highly contagious bacterial infection characterized by pink, water-filled raised lesions that develop a yellow crust and eventually rupture.

Inclusion Collection of chemical substances in cells, such as stored nutrients or cell products.

Inorganic Referring to compounds that are not organic; includes water, salts, minerals, and many acids and bases.

Integral protein A protein that is embedded within the lipid bilayer of a cell membrane.

Integumentary system Skin and its derivatives, forming the outer protective layer of the body.

Intermediate filament Cytoskeletal element that mechanically strengthens some cells.

Immediate hypersensitivity Allergic reaction that usually occurs within seconds or minutes of exposure to an allergen, mainly caused by histamine release from mast cells.

Interphase Interval between nuclear divisions when a cell increases in mass and duplicates is chromosomes.

Isotonic solution A fluid that has the same osmotic pressure as body fluids.

Jaundice A yellowish skin color resulting from excess bile pigments in the blood.

Keratin Tough, fibrous protein found in keratinocytes of the epidermis, hair, and nails.

Keratinocyte The majority cell type of epidermis that allows skin to be a protective barrier.

Kinetic energy Energy of motion.

Lacuna (plural: lacunae) a small cavity in bone and cartilage occupied by cells such as chondrocytes and osteocytes.

Langerhan's cell A type of macrophage found in the epidermis that ingests foreign particles.

Lanugo Soft, fine hair that covers a fetus.

Leukocyte A white blood cell.

Light microscope A device that uses a beam of light to magnify the image of a specimen.

Lipid Organic compound formed of carbon, hydrogen, and oxygen that is insoluble in water; a fat.

Lunula The whitish, crescent-moon-shaped area at the base of a nail.

Lysosome A vesicle that originates from the Golgi apparatus and contains digestive enzymes.

Malignant A term referring to tumors that can spread and invade surrounding tissues.

Major elements A group of four elements (carbon, hydrogen, oxygen, and nitrogen) that compose over 95% of the human body.

Male pattern baldness A genetically determined, sex-influenced loss of hair.

Glossary

Malignant Tumors that are capable of spreading by metastasis; cancerous.

Mammary gland Modified sweat glands, specialized to secrete milk.

Mast cell A type of white blood cell capable of releasing histamine and other inflammatory factors.

Matrix Actively dividing area of a follicle that forms hair.

Meiosis Two nuclear divisions that decrease the number of chromosomes in half, resulting in four daughter cells.

Melanin A pigment produced by melanocytes that gives color to skin and hair.

Melanocyte An epidermal skin cell that synthesizes and releases melanin.

Melanoma Cancer of melanocytes.

Merkel cell Sensory structure for touch found in the epidermis of skin.

Metabolism The sum total of all the chemical reactions occurring in the body.

Metaphase Second stage of mitosis where all the duplicated chromosomes line up at the equator of the spindle.

Metastasis The spread of cancer from one body part to another not directly connected.

Microfilament Cytoskeletal element that helps cells move and also maintain their shape.

Micrometer A unit of measurement equivalent to one millionth of a meter.

Microtubule Cytoskeletal element that plays a role in cell shape, growth, and motion.

Microvillus Tiny membrane projection on the apical surface of some epithelial cells.

Mitochondrion Organelle responsible for production of ATP.

Mitosis Nuclear division that results in an equal distribution of genetic material to each daughter cell.

Muscle tissue A tissue type capable of generating force by contracting.

Mutagen A substance or agent that can cause a change in the DNA base sequence.

Myelin sheath Insulating layer around neuronal axons formed from neuroglia.

Nail bed Layer of epithelium under a nail that is continuous with the stratum basale of skin.

Nanometer One billionth of a meter.

Necrosis Death of a cell or group of cells due to injury or disease.

Nervous tissue A tissue type that includes neurons and neuroglia.

Neuroglia Neural tissue cells that support, protect, and insulate neurons.

Neuron Neural tissue capable of generating and conducting impulses.

Nonpolar Molecules that are electrically balanced, uncharged.

Nuclear envelope A double-membrane barrier surrounding the nucleus.

Nuclear pore A channel in the nuclear envelope that is permeable to water and solutes, and regulates the transport of ribosomal subunits.

Nucleic acid Class of organic molecules that includes DNA and RNA.

Nucleolus (plural: nucleoli) Dense, spherical structure in the nucleus that is an assembly site for ribosomal subunits.

Nucleoplasm Gel-like fluid portion of a nucleus, enclosed by the nuclear envelope. Contains dissolved salts and nutrients.

Nucleus Control center of the cell, contains the genetic material (DNA) and separates DNA from the cytoplasm.

Oncogene Any gene having the potential to induce formation of cancer.

Organ A part of the body formed by two or more tissues and adapted to carry out a specific function (e.g., the kidney).

Organelles Small cellular structures in the cytoplasm that perform specific functions for the cell as a whole.

Organic Referring to molecules composed of carbon and hydrogen linked by covalent bonds, such as proteins, lipids, and carbohydrates.

Osmosis Diffusion of a solvent, such as water, through a membrane down its concentration gradient from a region of low solute concentration to one of higher concentration.

Glossary

Osmotic pressure Amount of pressure that is necessary to stop the flow of water by osmosis.

Osteocyte A mature bone cell.

Osteon Microscopic structure of compact bone consisting of an elongated cylinder composed of concentric rings of extracellular matrix called lamellae.

Papilla Nipple-like region of dermis that nourishes a growing hair.

Papillary layer The thinner outer layer of the dermis composed of loose connective tissue.

Passive transport Membrane transport processes that do not require cellular energy.

Peripheral protein A protein that is located on the outer or inner surface of a cell membrane.

Peroxisome A vesicle that detoxifies harmful substances, such as free radicals.

Phagocytosis Vesicular transport of solid particles.

Phosphate A molecular group consisting of one phosphorous and four oxygen atoms.

Pinocytosis Vesicular transport of particles dissolved in fluid.

Plasma The nonliving liquid portion of blood composed of water and various solutes.

Plasma membrane Outermost layer of a cell that forms a structural and functional boundary between the cytoplasm and the environment outside a cell.

Platelet Cell fragment that releases substances involved with blood clotting.

Polar Molecules that contain an electrical charge.

Port wine stain Red birthmark that contains an abnormally dense collection of dermal blood vessels, usually on the face or neck.

Prophase The first phase in mitosis where the duplicated genetic material condenses into chromosomes.

Protein Complex organic molecule containing carbon, hydrogen, oxygen, and nitrogen; composed of amino acids.

Protozoan Diverse group of single-celled organisms.

Pseudostratified epithelium A single layer of epithelial cells that has a multilayer appearance.

Receptor A membrane protein that has binding sites that will interact with specific extracellular molecules.

Resolution The ability to make separate parts look clear and distinguishable from one another.

Reticular lamina A layer of extracellular material, that is a major component of the basement membrane, secreted by connective tissue cells.

Reticular layer The thicker inner layer of the dermis composed of dense connective tissue.

Ribosome A non-membranous organelle that is the site of protein synthesis.

RNA (ribonucleic acid) A single-stranded macromolecule that carries out DNA's instructions for protein synthesis.

Rosacea Flushing of facial skin characterized by engorgement of blood vessels, especially of the cheeks and nose.

Scanning electron microscope An electron microscope that focuses a beam of electrons to reveal structure on the outer surface of a specimen.

Sebaceous gland Oil gland that secretes sebum, usually into a hair follicle.

Sebum Oily substance made of fats, cholesterol, protein, and salts that lubricates hair and skin.

Second-degree burn Burn with damage extending through the epidermis into the upper region of the dermis.

Selectively permeable The capacity of cell membranes to let some substances through but not others.

Semipermeable See selectively permeable.

Simple diffusion The unassisted transport of lipid-soluble substances across a cell membrane.

Simple epithelium Epithelial cells arranged in a single layer.

Glossary

Skeletal muscle A voluntary contractile tissue connected to bones, responsible for most body movements.

Smooth muscle A contractile tissue found in hollow organs and around blood vessels.

Solute Any substance dissolved in a solution.

Solute pump Protein carrier that mediates active transport of solutes across a cell membrane against their concentration gradients.

Solvent Any fluid, such as water, in which one or more substances are dissolved.

Spontaneous generation Refers to the concept that living organisms arise spontaneously from nonliving material, such as garbage.

Squamous Flat or scale-like.

Squamous cell carcinoma Skin cancer that arises from the keratinocytes of the stratum spinosum, usually on the scalp, ears, lower lip, and hands.

Stain A dye used to increase the contrast of cells for light microscopy.

Stem cell Undifferentiated cell possessing the potential to become any cell type.

Stratified epithelium Epithelial cells arranged in multiple layers.

Stratum basale Deepest layer of the epidermis whose cells are capable of active cell division.

Stratum corneum Outer layer of the epidermis, composed of flattened, dead, keratinized cells.

Stratum granulosum A layer of the epidermis composed of flattened cells containing keratohyalin, a substance that contributes to the formation of keratin.

Stratum lucidum A layer of flattened dead cells found in thick skin, such as the palms of the hands and soles of the feet.

Stratum spinosum Second deepest layer of the epidermis, containing cuboidal keratinocytes and scattered melanin granules and Langerhan's cells.

Subcutaneous Beneath the skin.

Subcutaneous tissue layer of connective tissue below skin; anchors skin, stores fat, and acts as thermal and mechanical insulation.

Sudiforous gland Epidermal gland that produces sweat.

Telomere Special cap on the end of chromosomes that protect them from fraying or fusing with other chromosomes.

Telophase Final phase of mitosis that begins when the chromosomes have migrated to the poles of the cells and ends with the complete separation of two daughter cells.

Terminal hair Thick, strong hair, such as that on the scalp, and the eyebrows and eyelashes.

Third-degree burn A burn that extends all the way through the epidermis and dermis into underlying subcutaneous tissues.

Tissue A group of similar cells and intercellular substances specialized to form a specific function.

Trace element Any element that makes up less than 0.01% of body weight.

Transitional epithelium Epithelium lining organs subject to considerable stretching.

Transmission electron microscope An electron microscope that focuses a beam of electrons through a specimen to reveal internal structure.

Tumor A tissue mass composed of cells that are dividing at an abnormally high rate; can be cancerous.

Tumor suppressor gene A gene that checks for proper DNA duplication; initiates apoptosis when damage to DNA is not repairable.

Vasoconstriction Narrowing of blood vessels due to contraction of smooth muscle located in blood vessel walls.

Vasodilation Relaxation of the smooth muscle of blood vessels, which leads to a widening of vessel diameter.

Vellis hair Soft and fine hair that persists throughout life and covers most of the body surface.

Vesicle A small, fluid-filled membranous sac.

Vesicular transport Movement of fairly large particles across cell membranes by enclosing them in vesicles during endocytosis and releasing them from vesicles during exocytosis.

Bibliography

Books and Journals

Ackerman, M.J. and D.E. Clapham. "Ion cannels: basic science and clinical disease." *Mechanisms of Disease* 336. (1997) 1575-1586.

Alberts, B., D. Bray, J. Lewis, M. Raff, K. Roberts, and J.D. Watson. *Molecular Biology of the Cell.* New York: Garland Publ. (1983) 1146.

Allison, A. "Lysosomes and Disease." *Scientific American* 217. (1967) 62-72.

Boon, T. "Teaching the Immune System to Fight Cancer." *Scientific American*, 263. (1993) 782-789.

Bretscher, M.S. "The Molecules of the Cell Membrane." *Scientific American*, 253. (1985) 100-108.

Byrne, J.H. and S.G. Schultz. *Introduction to Membrane Transport and Bioelectricity.* New York: Raven Press. (1988) 232.

Cavance, W.K. and R.L. White. "The Genetic Basis of Cancer." *Scientific American*, 272. (1995) 72-79.

Darnell, J., H. Lodish, and D. Baltimore. *Molecular Cell Biology*, 2nd ed., New York: Scientific American Books. (1986) 1187 .

Duke, R.C., D.M. Ojcius, and J.D. Young. "Cell Suicide in Health and Disease." *Scientific American* 275. (1996) 80-87.

Fischetti, M. "Tan or Burn." *Scientific American* 285. (2001) 90-91.

Golde, D.W. "The Stem Cell." *Scientific American* 265. (1991) 86-93.

Goodsell, D.S. "Inside a Living Cell." *Trends in Biochemistry.* 16. (1991) 203-206.

Greider, C.W. and E.H. Blackburn. "Telomeres, Telomerase, and Cancer." *Scientific American* 274. (1996) 92-97.

Haldane, J.B.S. *On Being the Right Size, in Possible Worlds and Other Essays.* London: Chatto and Windus. (1927) 18-26.

Hille, B. *Ionic Channels of Excitable Membranes*, 2nd ed., Sunderland, Mass.: Sinauer Publ. (1992) 607.

Ingber, D.E. "The Architecture of Life." *Scientific American* 278. (1998) 48-57.

Jablonksi, N.G. and G. Chaplin. "Skin Deep." *Scientific American* 287. (2002) 74-81.

Kinoshita, J. "The Oncogene Connection." *Scientific American* 262. (1990) 24-25.

Leffell, D.J. and D.E. Brash. "Sunlight and Skin Cancer." *Scientific American* 275. (1996) 52-59.

Lewis, T. *The Lives of a Cell: Notes.* New York: Bantam Books Inc. (1974) 180.

Lichenstein, L.M. "Allergy and the Immune System." *Scientific American* 269. (1993) 116-124.

Liotta, L.A. "Cancer Cell Invasion and Metastasis." *Scientific American* 266. (1992) 54-63.

Marguilis, L. and D. Sagan. *What is Life?* New York: Simon & Schuster. (1995).

Marieb, E. *Human Anatomy and Physiology.* 5th ed., San Francisco: Benjamin Cummings. (2001) 1248.

Mazia, D. "The Cell Cycle." *Scientific American* 230. (1974) 53-64.

Nicolaou, K.C., R.K. Guy, and P. Potier. "Taxoids: New Weapons Against Cancer." *Scientific American* 274. (1996) 94-98.

Pedersen, R. "Embryonic Stem Cells for Medicine." *Scientific American* 280. (1999) 68-73.

Pedersen, R.A. "Embryonic Stem Cells for Medicine." *Scientific American* 280. (1999) 68-73.

Rennie, J. "The Body Against Itself." *Scientific American* 263. (1990) 106-115.

Rothman, J.E. and L. Orci. "Budding Vesicles in Living Cells." *Scientific American* 274. (1996) 70-75.

Rusting, R.L. "Hair: Why it Grows and Why it Stops." *Scientific American* 284. (2001) 70-79.

Schmidt-Nielsen, K. *Scaling: Why is Animal Size so Important?* New York: Cambridge Univ. Press. (1989) 241.

Sharon, N. and H. Lis. "Carbohydrates in Cell Recognition." *Scientific American* 268. (1993) 82-89.

Singer, S.J. and G.L. Nicholson. "The Fluid Mosaic Model of the Structure of Cell Membranes." *Science* 175. (1972) 720-731.

Skou, J.C. "The Na-K Pump." *News in Physiological Sciences* 7. (1992) 95-100.

Stein, W.D. *Channels, Carriers, and Pumps: An Introduction to Membrane Transport.* New York: Academic Press. (1990) 326.

Stossel, T.P. "The Machinery of Cell Crawling." *Scientific American.* (Sept. 1994) 54-63.

Stryer, L. *Biochemistry,* 2nd ed.. San Francisco: W.H. Freeman & Co. (1981) 949.

Bibliography

Weinberg, R.A. "How Cancer Arises." *Scientific American* 275. (1996) 62-70.

Welsh, M.J. and A.E. Smith. "Cystic fibrosis." *Scientific American* 273. (1995) 52-59.

Wu, Crinna. "Unraveling the Mystery of Melanin: Does a Tan Protect Skin from Sun Damage or Contribute to it?" *Science News* 156. (1999) 190-191.

Websites

About microscopes:
http://www.microbeworld.org/htm/aboutmicro/tools/scopes.htm

Endosymbiosis:
http://users.rcn.com/jkimball.ma.ultranet/BiologyPages/E/Endosymbiosis.html

Jaundice in Newborns:
http://www.med.umich.edu/1libr/pa/pa_jaundnew_hhg.htm

Lysosomal Storage Diseases:
http://www.sas-centre.org/genetic/genpages/lysstodisindex.html

Source on electron microscopes:
http://www.unl.edu/CMRAcfem/em.htm

Source on stem cells:
http://www.nih.gov/news/stemcell/primer.htm

Structure and function of cell membranes:
http://users.rcn.com/jkimball.ma.ultranet/BiologyPages/C/CellMembranes.html

Tay Sachs Disease:
http://www.ninds.nih.gov/health_and_medical/disorders/taysachs_doc.htm

Telomerase, aging, and cancer:
http://www.genethik.de/telomerase.htm

The American Cancer Society homepage:
http://www.cancer.org/docroot/home/index.asp

Books and Journals

Alberts, B., D. Bray, A. Johnson, J. Lewis, M. Raff, K. Roberts, and P. Walter. *Essential Cell Biology: An Introduction to the Molecular Biology of the Cell.* New York: Garland Publ. (1998) 630.

Appell, D. "Getting Under Your Skin." *Scientific American* 288. (2003) 18-20.

Bayley, H. "Building Doors Into Cells." *Scientific American* 277. (1997) 62-67.

Beardsley, T. "Getting wired. New observations may show how neurons form connections." *Scientific American* 280. (1999) 24-26.

Beardsley, T. "Stem Cells Come of Age." *Scientific American* 281. (1999) 30-31.

Bretscher. M.S. "How Animal Cells Move." *Scientific American* 257. (1987) 89-90.

Buiseret, P.D. "Allergy." *Scientific American* 247. (1982) 86-95.

Caplan, A.I. "Cartilage." *Scientific American* 251. (1984) 90-94.

Cavenee, W.K. and R.L. White. "The Genetic Basis of Cancer." *Scientific American* 272. (1995) 72-79.

Chiras, D.D. *Human Biology: Health, Homeostasis, and the Environment.* 2nd ed. New York: West Publ. Co. (1995) 605.

Christensen, T., A. Moller-Larsen, and S. Haahr. "A retroviral implication in multiple sclerosis." *Trends in Microbiology* 2. (1994) 332-336.

Dean, G. "The Multiple Sclerosis Problem." *Scientific American* 223. (1970) 40-46.

Edelson, R.L. and J.M. Fink. "The Immunologic Function of Skin." *Scientific American* 252. (1985) 46-53.

Ezzell, C. "Starving Tumors of Their Lifeblood." *Scientific American* 279. (1998) 33-34.

Feldman, M. and L. Eisenbach. "What Makes a Tumor Cell Metastatic?" *Scientific American* 259. (1988) 60-65.

Hayflick, L. "The Cell Biology of Human Aging." *Scientific American* 242. (1980) 58-65.

Johnson, M.D. *Human Biology: Concepts and Current Issues.* San Francisco: Benjamin Cummings Publ. (2001) 563.

Kosta, L. "Multiplesensitivities." *Scientific American* 269. (1993) 10.

Laxarides, E. and J.P. Revel. "The Molecular Basis of Cell Movement." *Scientific American* 240. (1979) 100-113.

Further Reading

Leffell, D.J. and D.E. Brash. "Sunlight and Skin Cancer." *Scientific American* 275. (1996) 52-59.

Martindale, D. "Scar No More." *Scientific American* 283. (2000) 34-36.

Morell, P. and W.T. Norton. "Myelin." *Scientific American* 242. (1980) 88-90.

Neher, E. and B. Sakmann. "The Patch Clamp Technique." *Scientific American* 266. (1992) 44-51.

Nucci, M.L. and A. Abuchowski. "The Search for Blood Substitutes." *Scientific American* 278. (1998) 72-77.

Oliff, A., J.B. Gibbs, and F. McCormick. "New Molecular Targets for Cancer Therapy." *Scientific American* 275. (1996) 144-149.

Parenteau, N. "Skin: The First Tissue-Engineered Products." *Scientific American* 280. (1999) 83-84.

Rose, M.R. "Can Human Aging Be Postponed?" *Scientific American* 281. (1999) 106-111.

Ross, R. and P. Bornstein. "Elastic Fibers in the Body." *Scientific American* 224. (1971) 44-52.

Rothman, J.E. "The Compartmental Organization of the Golgi Apparatus." *Scientific American* 253. (1985) 74-89.

Saladin, K. *Anatomy and Physiology*, 2nd ed. New York: McGraw Hill. (2001) 1115.

Shier, D., J. Butler, and R. Lewis. *Essentials of Human Anatomy and Physiology*, 6th ed., Boston: WCB McGraw Hill. (1998) 617.

Websites

About light microscopes:
http://www.ruf.rice.edu/~bioslabs/methods/microscopy/microscopy.html

Acne organization:
http://www.acne.org/

Acne, American Academy of Dermatology:
http://www.aad.org/pamphlets/acnepamp.html

American Academy of Dermatology, Skin Cancer:
http://www.aad.org/SkinCancerNews/WhatIsSkinCancer/

An introduction to skin cancer:
http://www.maui.net/~southsky/introto.html#how

Cell cycle and mitosis tutorial:
http://www.biology.arizona.edu/cell_bio/tutorials/cell_cycle/main.html

Cell organelle structure and function:
http://www.tvdsb.on.ca/westmin/science/sbi3a1/Cells/cells.htm

Exocrine and endocrine glands:
http://www.mhhe.com/biosci/ap/histology_mh/glands.html

Fact sheet about skin cancer:
http://www.cdc.gov/cancer/nscpep/skin.htm

How cells function:
http://science.howstuffworks.com/cell1.htm

How light microscopes work:
http://science.howstuffworks.com/light-microscope.htm

How scanning electron microscopes function:
http://www.mos.org/sln/SEM/

Images of cells and organelles, cell cycle, mitosis:
http://www.cellsalive.com/

Ion channels and membrane transport:
http://www.omedon.co.uk/ionchan/

Membrane structure and transport:
*http://www.emc.maricopa.edu/faculty/farabee/BIOBK/
BioBooktransp.html*

Pictures of epithelial tissues:
http://www.uoguelph.ca/zoology/devobio/210labs/epithelial1.html

Skin and connective tissue diseases:
http://www.mic.ki.se/Diseases/c17.html

Structure and function of cell membranes:
http://cellbio.utmb.edu/cellbio/membrane.htm

Teaching unit on diffusion and osmosis:
http://biology.arizona.edu/sciconn/lessons/mccandless/default.html

Telomeres and telomerase:
http://avsunxsvr.aeiveos.com/agethry/telomere/

The nucleus:
http://cellbio.utmb.edu/cellbio/nucleus.htm

Conversion Chart

Unit (metric)		Metric to English		English to Metric	
LENGTH					
Kilometer	km	1 km	0.62 mile (mi)	1 mile (mi)	1.609 km
Meter	m	1 m	3.28 feet (ft)	1 foot (ft)	0.305 m
Centimeter	cm	1 cm	0.394 inches (in)	1 inch (in)	2.54 cm
Millimeter	mm	1 mm	0.039 inches (in)	1 inch (in)	25.4 mm
Micrometer	μm				
WEIGHT (MASS)					
Kilogram	kg	1 kg	2.2 pounds (lbs)	1 pound (lbs)	0.454 kg
Gram	g	1 g	0.035 ounces (oz)	1 ounce (oz)	28.35 g
Milligram	mg				
Microgram	μg				
VOLUME					
Liter	L	1 L	1.06 quarts	1 gallon (gal)	3.785 L
				1 quart (qt)	0.94 L
				1 pint (pt)	0.47 L
Milliliter	mL or cc	1 mL	0.034 fluid ounce (fl oz)	1 fluid ounce (fl oz)	29.57 mL
Microliter	μL				
TEMPERATURE					
°C = 5/9 (°F − 32)		°F = 9/5 (°C + 32)			

Index

Index

Index

Picture Credits

About the Author

Douglas B. Light is an accomplished educator, and holds degrees in biology (B.A.), zoology (M.S.), and physiology (Ph.D.). His academic career began at Winslow High School in Maine where he taught biology. He joined the faculty at Ripon College in 1989 and taught general biology, anatomy and physiology, and immunology. He is presently Professor of Biology at Lake Forest College, where he teaches courses in organismal biology and animal physiology. He also conducts research designed to elucidate the mechanisms regulating transport of substances across biological membranes and how cells maintain their proper size. He has received over a half dozen awards for his teaching and research excellence, and has been the recipient of several major grants from the National Science Foundation. He has published over a dozen articles in scientific journals and has presented his research findings at numerous scientific conferences. Light is a member of several scientific and professional organizations, including the American Physiological Society, the Society for Integrative & Comparative Biology, and the Society of General Physiologists.